A WAR IN
1943-1945

TRUE ADVENTURES
IN ENEMY TERRITORY

MALCOLM TUDOR, BSc.

EMILIA PUBLISHING

ISBN 9780953896448

6511848000
940.5421

First published in 2007 by

EMILIA PUBLISHING

Woodlands, Bryn Gardens, Newtown,
Powys, SY16 2DR, United Kingdom

www.emiliapublishing.com

To: my readers

ACKNOWLEDGEMENTS

I would like to thank veterans of the war in Italy and their relatives who have provided me with information.

Special thanks to George Almond, Ted Fry, John Langrishe, Albert Materazzi, Bill Steed, Anne Storm, and my friends in Italy.

Photographs kindly contributed by:

George Almond, Ted Fry, John Langrishe and Anne Storm.

OTHER BOOKS BY MALCOLM TUDOR

'British Prisoners of War in Italy: Paths to Freedom'
(2000)

'Escape from Italy, 1943-45: Allied Escapers and Helpers
in Fascist Italy' (2003)

'Special Force: SOE and the Italian Resistance
1943-1945' (2004)

'Prisoners and Partisans: Escape and Evasion
in World War II Italy' (2006)

Available directly from Emilia Publishing
by post or online:

Woodlands, Bryn Gardens, Newtown,
Powys, SY16 2DR, United Kingdom

www.emiliapublishing.com

Or through booksellers

Contents

Introduction

On 10 June 1940 Italy declared war on Great Britain and France. Both Italy and Germany announced they were at war with the United States on 11 December 1941. Just over 20 months later, the Allies invaded southern Italy.

Before dawn on 3 September 1943, the Eighth Army attacked from Sicily across the Straits of Messina in Operation Baytown. A vast number of landing craft and small ships laden with troops crossed under the protection of an aerial and naval bombardment. The first landing on the mainland of Hitler's Europe was achieved with little opposition.

Later on the same day, the unconditional surrender of the Italian Armed Forces was accepted in an olive grove at Cassibile in Sicily. The armistice was kept secret until five days later.

The main Allied landing took place at Salerno on 9 September in Operation Avalanche. The British 10th and US 6th corps under General Mark Clark established the bridgehead in the face of stiff opposition. Meanwhile, the British 1st Airborne Division went ashore at Taranto.

Naples fell to the Allies on 1 October with the help of a popular rising. The campaign had begun well.

However, instead of withdrawing to the Alps as anticipated, the German Army created a strong defensive position south of Rome, the Gustav Line, and relied on adverse weather, the steep mountains and swift rivers to help halt the Allied advance.

The dictator Mussolini was rescued by German special forces from a ski lodge in the Abruzzo mountains on 12 September. He was installed as head of the Italian Social Republic, based at Salò on Lake Garda. Fascism had returned, no longer royalist, and crueller.

For the people of Naples the second phase of the war lasted 23 days. But in central Italy it was nine months before Rome was liberated on 4 June 1944. And 20 months were to elapse before the cities of the north were freed at the end of April 1945.

Among the liberators was my father, Quartermaster Sergeant Kenneth Winston Tudor, of the Royal Corps of Signals, who went with the Eighth Army from Sicily to the Alps - and found a wife in the process, my mother.

The guns at last fell silent on 2 May 1945. Allied troops had just reached the Brenner Pass and Trieste.

This book is a tribute to all the servicemen and resisters who helped free Italy. It is a pleasure to tell their story.

The *Centro Cardinal Ferrari*, Fontanellato, now a private medical centre, wartime Camp 49 for Allied prisoners of war (author's photograph).

1 Freedom

The changing tide of war in September 1943 brought early release for thousands of Allied prisoners of war (POWs) in Italy. Most of the men had been captured in North Africa, some more than three years earlier.

At the time of the Armistice there were 80,000 captives scattered in camps across the centre and north of the peninsula. Just over 85 per cent of the servicemen were from Great Britain and the British Empire and Commonwealth of Nations, with the others mainly American, French, Greek, Russian and Yugoslav.

A secret message, dated 7 June 1943, had been sent to every Senior British Officer (SBO), or his equivalent, ordering them to ensure that 'prisoners of war remain within camp' in the event of the Allied invasion of Italy.

Many of the men followed the 'stand fast order' and as a result were captured by the Germans and sent by train to camps in Greater Germany. In contrast, in the few large camps where the leader disobeyed the command - and at most work camps - the majority of the captives escaped.

The most famous camp whose inmates were liberated was PG 49 Fontanellato in the province of Parma. There were 536 servicemen at PG 49, made up of 483 officers and 53 'other ranks' orderlies. This was the camp of origin of the prisoners of war helped by my mother and grandparents, Clara, Alfredo and Giuseppina Dall' Arda from the village of Castell' Arquato. I have been in frequent contact with many of the escapers from Fontanellato. This is the story of one of them.

Twenty-six-year-old Lieutenant John Langrishe of the Royal Artillery was captured by the Germans in June 1942 in Libya. In September he arrived at his first permanent POW camp in Italy, PG 41 Montalbo, a small medieval castle near Piacenza. The camp was closed in the spring of 1943 and the prisoners transferred to nearby PG 49, housed in the newly built orphanage at Fontanellato.

In this fine account, John Langrishe recalls the events on the announcement of the Armistice on 8 September 1943:

I had come back to my room after supper and was chatting with two or three others when the serenity of the summer evening was shattered by a growing hubbub from the direction of the village. We went to the windows and soon were astonished to see a large crowd of the villagers, joined by our guards, come hurrying down the road, some on bicycles and some on foot, shouting, singing, cheering and throwing their caps in the air. 'Peace, peace,' they cried. The soldiers flung down their rifles, jumped on them, and called out to us that we were now their friends.

Our first reaction was one of numbness. Here was the thing we had all been waiting for, and what were we to do? Were we free to leave the camp? Would our troops be with us in the morning? How would we be sent home? These and a hundred other like questions sprang into our minds until through the chatter of excited conversation came the order that the Senior British Officer (SBO), Lieutenant Colonel Hugo De Burgh, would address all ranks in the main hall immediately.

The crowd of some five hundred excited prisoners thronged into the hall and we heard the SBO make his announcement. It was indeed true that the Italian Government had surrendered unconditionally to the Allies and that we should, in the normal course of events, expect to be speedily repatriated.

He explained that all ranks must remain in camp until further orders and that the Italian commandant, Lieutenant Colonel Eugenio Vicedomini, had made arrangements with him for the speedy evacuation of the camp if it became necessary. The SBO wound up by saying that, unless any emergency arose, nothing further would take place until nine the following morning, when another full parade would be held.

We all retired to our rooms, where every sort of discussion ranged back and forth upon the situation and the future course of events. It was confidently assumed that there would soon be Allied landings in the Gulf of Genoa, mainly in order that the large number of prisoner of war camps in the plain should be released. There must have been nearly fifty thousand prisoners spread over quite a small area. But alas, how wrong were these estimates.

At dawn, the Italian guards on the gates were replaced by our own 'police' and after breakfast all ranks fell in for the muster parade. It was a great occasion, our first parade at which no Italians had been present. The SBO gave out his orders in the shortest possible time. All ranks were to don battledress, collect one day's hard rations, and then be ready to evacuate the camp at five minutes notice on the sounding of a bugle borrowed from the Italians. Further orders would be announced later.

This was all soon done. We made our rooms tidy and parcelled up and packed away those things we would have to leave behind in case they could be recovered at a later date. Small knots of people formed, exchanging addresses and giving messages for those at home in the event of trouble on the way.

Somehow it seemed unreal that after all these long months, in many cases years, the great day had come and we would once more be going forth free men into the outer world; unreal that the tables were turned, that we were now the bosses and the Italians dancing to our tune; and unreal that this large and ugly building, for so long our home from home, was now a place to be left behind as soon as possible.

Our thoughts also turned to those at home. What had they been told, and what did they expect us to be doing? In the events that were to follow, it turned out that their hopes were to be sorely tried. But just then we felt some of the happiness that they must have been feeling and we tried to picture our homes and friends in England.

Eleven o'clock was the signal for the usual mid-morning drink. We gathered in the stony courtyard at the rear of the building to receive our cocoa. Suddenly there was a roar of aeroplane engines and two black German Ju-88 bombers were to be seen streaking for the camp at low altitude over the fields. We thought this was the beginning of some sort of attack. The Germans knew where we were and we could not believe that they would let the chance of collecting several hundred British officer prisoners slip through their fingers. However, all was well and the planes passed safely overhead.

We then noticed that the Italians had cut away a long stretch of the wire at the end of the playing field. Freedom began to seem very sweet and near and beckoning.

Word went round that the Italian commandant had given orders to the guards that in the event of a German attempt to recapture us, they would defend the camp to the last man, or at any rate until we had made our escape. This did not inspire any great confidence in us, but in the present state of tension it showed that the commandant was on our side.

Midday had hardly sounded from our clock, and it was nearly time for lunch, when those in the rooms in the front of the building heard a cry they were to hear often in the days to follow: *'I Tedeschi vengono!'* the Germans are coming! I never knew whether our bugle sounded or not, but the desired effect was achieved with speed and efficiency.

Whilst gathering together my few belongings which I had put aside for this moment, I saw through the window the Italians putting into effect their promise to hold the camp.

It seemed that a small party of Germans had been seen some miles away. The rumour grew with repetition till I believe the Italians thought they were going to face an Army Corps. The officer of the guard was buckling on his pistol and steel helmet and at the same time crying to his men to fall in. They showed no great enthusiasm to do this and they were still less anxious to climb into the anti-escape ditch that had been dug to a depth of four feet round the perimeter wire. The officer, swearing the foulest oaths and gesticulating, picked up handfuls of pebbles and hurled them at his mutinous troops in fury. This, as might be expected, had no effect beyond making certain that they would desert at the earliest opportunity, which indeed they did some five minutes later.

Grabbing my small bundle, I went outside with the others to the playing field, where already platoons and companies were being marshalled. In a matter of five minutes the roll was called and the order to move off given. Almost with the precision of a trained formation, the columns of officers and 'other ranks,' carrying packs, cases and other equipment, moved away in threes to the left, through the gap and into the fields at the back of the village. At last we were out, free from the restraint of the Italians and responsible for our own actions and steps, but where would they lead us?

It was a beautiful sunny early autumn day as the column turned its back upon the camp and directed its feet across the stubble and onto the road running past the village. It was not long before the locals saw what was going on and came out of the houses to watch and wave and wish us luck. It was also not long before an Italian along the roadside was recognised as one of our guards. It had taken him no longer to demobilise himself than was required to change into civilian clothes and slip away from the huts. All was silent behind us in the camp, nor were there the expected sounds of shooting to be heard.

With us as we marched out to freedom came our two interpreter officers. The senior, Captain Camino, had practised as a metallurgical consultant in Sheffield before the war and was strongly Anglophile.

Much earlier in the day, one of the senior officers, Lieutenant Colonel Hugh Mainwaring, had made a reconnaissance for places to hide if such an eventuality as this should occur. It was to one of these hideouts that our way led. Through the village, down a lane and across the fields we went, a river of khaki in the sunny Italian countryside, till at last we came to the embankment along a small river. It was decided that we should remain there for the present. We all kept together but concealed ourselves behind the dyke and among the many clumps of bushes that grew there.

During the remainder of the day a small party was sent back to the camp to gather information. It appeared that some 10 or 15 minutes after the last POW had filed through the gap in the wire, one or two lorry loads of Germans arrived and entered the camp. They found the Italian commandant in his office with some of his officers, who told them that the English had gone. Their furious reaction was to place the Italians under arrest and then go through the building to see what they could find.

There now occurred a series of events which surprisingly demonstrated how German discipline can be less than effective if the temptation is strong enough. Though their prey had slipped through their fingers, the German soldiers did themselves very well on the lunch that was ready for eating when the camp was evacuated, on the store of wine that was our day's ration and on the Red Cross parcel stock. This they systematically looted together with our large tobacco store, before they sold the rest to the villagers for what they could get.

The remains of most of the parcels soon found their way out to us in our hide, brought by the locals whose sympathies were now very much on our side. Having done their worst, the Germans settled down to a torpid and drunken slumber in the camp before taking their departure some time later. In this way the Germans undoubtedly threw away their first and best chance of recapturing their quarry, when we were all together and close to the camp.

The day wore on and, in spite of the precautions taken to disguise our presence by the river, a steadily growing stream of Italians came across the fields bringing the remnants of our looted parcels to us. The two English-speaking Italian officers who had accompanied us visited the village and on their return confirmed what had occurred at the camp when the Germans came, and

5

added that the commandant and some of his officers had been taken away as prisoners.

As soon as darkness fell on this exciting day, the order arrived that we were to move again in case the Germans came upon us during the night. So we set off in files by platoons and companies southwards along the course of the river before settling down for the night, without blankets, under the bushes and trees that lined the banks of the stream.

Although I had brought my greatcoat with me, I found myself steadily growing colder as the night wore on, but in the end managed to get a few hours broken sleep on the hard ground. I woke up cold and stiff with the first light of morning. We made the best breakfast we could out of the tinned food that we had brought with us and then took stock of the situation. In a short while, even though everyone remained hidden, the locals found us and were soon regaling us joyfully with quite unbelievable news items supposedly heard on the radio.

Scouts were posted in all directions and then we all settled down for the day to see what the future would bring. The most immediate result was the report that the Allies had landed in the Gulf of Genoa. Whether this was wishful thinking on the part of the Italians, history does not relate, but as far as we were concerned it meant that our SBO's plans were fortunately laid as this was the eventuality that had been hoped for. Later in the day these reports were proved to be false, so he decided that as soon as it was dark enough we should all move south across the Via Emilia and make for the comparative safety of the mountains. But the lieutenant colonel added that as the position was so uncertain, he would not forbid the departure of small parties from the column if they wished to make their own way from then on.

As soon as dusk fell, my platoon moved off in single file through the bushes and thickets beside the river and past Italian farmhouses sleeping under a brilliant starry sky. Though our tread was made with the utmost care, it was not long before the first dog was awakened and a canine chorus rose to the heavens. It was taken up by one dog after another and passed from farm to farm as we stumbled through the night. This performance did not entirely rebound to our disadvantage. No doubt the Italians thought the walkers through the night were the hated German soldiers and they kept well within their doors.

Progress was slow and when I was approached by two friends from my own regiment, Mac and Jerry, with the suggestion that we make off on our own, I fell in with them. After telling our platoon commander of our intentions, we struck off to the east across the fields with the intention of putting as much distance between the main body and ourselves as possible before dawn. We trudged on for some two miles or so and when we thought that we were in open country settled down for a short sleep in a convenient dry ditch.

As soon as it became light, Mac, who could speak the best Italian, went off to a farm we could see a couple of hundred yards away over the fields to ask whether we could have food and shelter. He was received with great suspicion and finally returned from his mission unsuccessful.

We made what meal we could from the tinned food we still had with us. We found that we were in a vineyard and so were able to refresh ourselves with the near ripe fruit. As the sun rose in another cloudless sky we lay discussing what should be done. Early in the afternoon a peasant came past our hiding place and we plucked up the necessary courage to ask him for help.

He said he would ask the farmer whose house was at the top of the field and in a few minutes we saw him coming back. We were to go to the farm after dark and would be given food and lodging for the time being. So, when the sun had set on a day which seemed to have had many times the proper quantity of hours, we rose from our ditch and went to the house. We walked in single file and some yards distant from each other in case there should be a betrayal. But all was well.

The farmer and his wife, a weather-beaten couple of some 60 summers, made us welcome in their manner and soon we were sitting down to a magnificent plateful of steaming broth. Though the daytime was hot, the nights were growing chilly with the touch of oncoming autumn, and the hot soup drove the damp from our bones in a heartening way. It was also our first hot meal since supper three days previously. Our host showed us into the guests' bedroom, a warm, congenial hayloft where we spent a pleasant night, sleeping well and relaxed after the nervous tension of the preceding days.

For the next week we remained at this farm, which we found was only some three miles from the camp. Many tales reached us and we made contact with small groups of other ex-prisoners who were residing on nearby farms. It turned out that most of the main group had split into small parties and were laying up in the neighbourhood till reliable news was received which would enable them to form useful plans. The farmer would not have us on the premises during daylight, so we would go into the fields and meet our friends, taking a loaf and wine with us and passing the days in that manner. As soon as it became dark, we would return to our hot meal.

When we got to know our hosts better, a discussion would follow in our stilted but steadily improving Italian. They were anxious to learn of the English way of living, what our previous histories had been and what we thought would be the outcome of the war. The German radio kept announcing that Italians who were harbouring British prisoners would suffer heavily for their folly. Before this announcement, there had been one offering substantial rewards for information leading to the recapture of ex-prisoners. This had evoked no response, so threats were tried, which had even less success if that were possible.

There was, however, someone in the village with pro-German feelings, for information was given which led to the searching of one house reputed to harbour a British officer. It did indeed shelter one, but fortunately he was able to speak the language like a native.

The German search party came to the house and, as the owners were away in the fields, the British officer opened the door to them. One of the Germans spoke a little Italian and when he said that he was looking for a British officer, he was invited to make a thorough search of the house. From cellar to attic the party went, probing and seeking. They were assured that their informant had been mistaken and after some time they all departed from whence they came.

Few Germans bothered to learn Italian, so that they were usually unable to discern when they were speaking to an Englishman who spoke Italian with a fair degree of confidence, and thus often missed a capture they would otherwise have made. The story of this search soon spread through the village and their estimation of the British was greatly raised.

Our hosts now began to be rather jumpy and kept asking when we intended to leave, but we tried to put off the evil day as long as possible. One of our main difficulties, now that we were speedily overcoming the language problem, was procuring civilian clothes, without which it would not be safe for us to move about during daylight. We asked our host if he could fix us up. But as we were all larger than the normal run of Italians, he was not able to. Further, there was a big demand for such clothes from all those other escapees in the neighbourhood, and there were many extraordinary outfits to be seen. The family did however suggest that if it would be of any help they could dye our shirts and trousers blue or brown, which kind offer was accepted.

The next day they borrowed some ill-fitting clothing for us while our shirts were dyed brown and our trousers blue. We still had no jackets other than our battledress, but they would have to do for the present. When our things were dry, we found that we were not nearly so conspicuous as before and that we were well clad in the bargain. We compared very favourably with the stage bandit appearance of some of our friends in their borrowed plumes.

Footwear was also a problem. I decided to retain my army boots for the long walk that I foresaw that I would have to make, even though they were easily recognisable by sharp-eyed Germans.

My host intimated that we might advantageously find other accommodation, so I scouted around the already overcrowded neighbourhood for another farm. Jerry and Mac agreed that under the circumstances it would be better to split.

On 20 September, with my few belongings on my back, I went to the farm of one Maestri at the village of Toccalmatto, about one and a half miles from Fontanellato. It was a much larger and more modern farm, but there was as usual a fly in the ointment. To be more accurate, there were millions. They crawled up the walls in their thousands and over the food in their hundreds, flying from dung-heap to kitchen and back with the greatest impartiality and frequency.

Maestri and his family welcomed me. I was given the luxury of a separate bedroom, a change from the draughty loft in which we had previously been sleeping. In return for my keep, I said I would be happy to help on the farm. I was taken at my word and found a new experience in my life.

Since I had left the camp the weather had been more than kind. There had been a succession of those days that are the foreigners' conception of sunny Italy. The Plain of Lombardy shimmered in the dusty heat of the late summer and the distant Alps hung like a backcloth of dream mountains across the horizon. Daily the air was filled with a procession of vast and cumbrous Messerschmitt transport planes, and a never ending stream of vehicles paraded back and forth along the main road two miles away. Horrid tales were told of the bodies of Italians lying on the road, crushed by the tracks of Hitler's tanks, and all the while the grapes swelled on the vines and purpled in the hot sun in anticipation of the coming harvest.

My day was well arranged. In the mornings I would help on the farm, lifting sugar beet, a backbreaking job, or muck-spreading, which was an equally tiring form of entertainment. Then, after a generous lunch of pasta and rough red wine, I would go over the fields to where a small group of my friends would meet to spend the afternoon in speculation as to the trend of events and making plans for returning to our own homes. By now we had come to the conclusion that if we were to wait for the arrival of our troops, we might be there till doomsday. The consensus of opinion was for a move: some said to Switzerland and some to the south, but understandably no one was anxious to leave their comfortable billets for the uncertainty of the open country.

Then the weather broke and for several days it was impossible to work in the fields. As the grapes had been harvested, all hands on the farm were turned to the task of making the wine. Basket after basket of fine black grapes would be emptied into the large trough for pressing. I was entreated to take my turn, without boots, in the trough, but said I was unskilled and would prefer to lift the tubs of grape juice from the trough to the vats. This was, as it turned out, a far more exhausting job than I had anticipated.

Sometimes I would be engaged in conversation by the farmer's daughters, children of eight and nine, who were always much intrigued by the few English books that I had managed to bring with me and were avid for information about the British Isles. I explained that they were situated away to the north of their sunny land, that there was more rain and fog and that it was much colder. I told them of Wales and Ireland and Scotland, whereupon they assured me that Scotland was an island inhabited by a barbaric people who did not even have windows in their houses. My efforts to correct them were received with doubt. Could this grotesque distortion of the facts have been the work of the Fascist teaching? In between these conversations, they made the day hideous with their continuous fighting and screaming, so that it was a joy to be out of the house in the open fields.

By this time I was getting anxious about what I was to do, and though I was inclined to make for Switzerland I could not bring myself to the point of setting out. In the end, action was forced upon me.

Shortly after the misty dawn of 29 September, I was woken by a battering on my door, which opened to reveal Maestri on the threshold in a great state of alarm. The village *Carabiniere*, the policeman, had just rushed in with the news that the Germans had begun a large-scale sweep of the neighbourhood with special forces and that I would be well advised to make a getaway into the fields. I pieced this news together from the almost incoherent spate of Italian that fell from his lips and was then almost forcibly propelled out of the house with a crust in my hand and told to take cover in a nearby ditch.

After a little while, as the coast seemed clear, I made my way across the fields to spend the rest of the day in discussion with a group of my friends who had received similar treatment from their hosts. It seemed that there was really something in this story. We came to the conclusion that the neighbourhood was getting too hot to hold us and that in any case it was not right to outstay the welcome that we had enjoyed from the simple Italian farming folk. We therefore made plans for the morrow.

Four of us would start early and, for the present, make for the town of Bardi in the mountains to the south, where we were told there were many friendly Italians. My friend Buck, who was to be one of the four, returned with me to Maestri's farm that night.

Our host only took us in with the greatest reluctance, but finally we were put in the hayloft, a big come down after my luxurious bedroom. He seemed to be appeased when we assured him that we would be gone for good the next day. I was a bit concerned about how to follow our route, as the only map I had been able to obtain was a tiny one torn from the pages of an elementary school atlas belonging to one of the children, but it was better than none at all.

The other officers in the escape party were Captain David Buchanan (Buck) and Lieutenant John Eadie, both also in the Royal Artillery, and Lieutenant VA Buist (Bunny) of the Royal Armoured Corps (RAC). The escape attempt would begin at dawn.

John Langrishe, Cairo, 1940.

2 The Long Walk Out

After the war, British gunnery lieutenant and escaper John Langrishe recalled the start of his journey through enemy territory:

The morning of 30 September dawned fine but misty after a peaceful night free from alarms. We were given an early breakfast and almost before we had finished, the other two arrived. We then set out across the fields, Buck, John, Bunny and myself, wondering what the future had in store for us and where our steps would turn.

We travelled light and fast through the damp fields and past the farms whose occupants were hardly astir. We planned to skirt west of Fidenza, where there was reputed to be a German garrison, and to strike into the hills after crossing the railway and main road. We had already learned that the Germans seldom strayed from an important road or a large town and this knowledge was to prove of inestimable value in the days to come.

After about three hours march, we came upon the railway. We were travelling along a deep streambed which we found running straight towards the line. Crawling and fighting our way through the thick undergrowth, we passed safely under the track.

At the very outset of our journey we did not feel inclined to run any unnecessary risks, so chose a long brick drain as our means of passing under the road. I was leading the procession. On coming out into the daylight at the far end through a thick hedge, I found myself face to face with an Italian peasant. Who was the more surprised I cannot say, but he did not hinder us as we cut away across the fields.

It may seem that we were taking somewhat excessive precautions. But it must be borne in mind that we had no intention of being recaptured through carelessness, and that we had good reason from the military point of view to expect bridges to be guarded or under some kind of supervision. In fact, there were usually no guards.

As we left the road behind, we joined a country track running upwards and southwards along the crest of a ridge past some large but dilapidated houses. We could see that even in the course of a mile or so we had risen quite considerably above the level of the plain in which we had passed the previous five months. We could also observe for the first time the extent of the military traffic on the main road, the Via Emilia. On our right in a narrow valley ran a metalled highway, but there was no sign of life on it with the exception of an occasional farm cart. Ahead of us rose the main ridge of the Apennines, fir-clad and sparsely inhabited.

The day was drawing on and there was no immediate prospect of a night's shelter. Owing to the easy life we had been leading, we were all suffering in varying degrees from soreness of the feet and were extremely tired. We had already covered 12 or more miles of hard going without much food. Soon we were passing a large camp of huts among the fir trees. As we saw there were German troops moving about, we had to drive our flagging bodies yet further, for no Italian would take us in with the enemy in such proximity. In the end, we finally dragged ourselves another couple of miles along the mule track we were following and entered the village of Vigoleno, nestling among the hills.

We asked for shelter at the first house and luck was with us. We were made right royally welcome and invited in by the farmer, a well-to-do man with a prosperous looking house. In what seems less time than to tell of it, we were sitting down at a well-covered table to a magnificent supper. Our host offered a choice of a more than palatable red or white sparkling wine. When I remarked that this seemed a very fine drink, he replied that before the war it had been exported and was quite well known.

The meal over, we were all taken to the house of an old couple in the village who had spent many years in England and had many fond memories of the country. They gave us an even warmer welcome, if that were possible, and a glass of excellent wine. They told us of their son who was still in England and of whom they had received no news for years. We were given messages to carry home from this heartbroken couple. There followed the ceremony of listening to the nine o'clock news broadcast in Italian from the BBC, a custom we found had even been widely observed during the Mussolini regime, despite the heavy penalties. We returned to our farm with a tearful farewell and Godspeed from the aged pair. It was in its way very touching to find Italians so pro-English.

Our bedroom was the familiar hayloft. As the night was turning cold, we burrowed well down into the hay and gave our aching bones and muscles the rest for which they had been crying out for so long. The depth of our sleep proved that a comfortable bed is an unnecessary luxury if one is healthily tired.

We awoke to the sound of raindrops falling on the roof of our loft. Unless we were willing to get very wet, we would have to delay our start till the weather cleared. So we took stock of our possessions as our chore before lunch.

I was travelling in my blue-dyed slacks and brown-dyed shirt with my battle dress blouse and army issue boots. I had a razor and strop, shaving brush, towel, four handkerchiefs and three pairs of spare socks. I was also carrying a new travelling alarm clock, carefully wrapped in a piece of linen, which I had bought in Fontanellato as a 21st birthday present for my brother at home. It was a Swiss clock purchased with hard-earned lire from my POW 'pay' and I imagined it was something unlikely to be obtainable in wartime UK. To these must be added my diary and the map, and my list of possessions is complete. There was a lot to be said for travelling light.

We each had a minimum of a hundred lire, which had been issued before we left the camp for use in emergencies. I also had my Middle East officers' identity card, which later proved of great use.

The lunch we were given was an even finer meal than that offered the night before. There was roast duck as the main course, liberally washed down with the red and white wine to which we had been introduced at the previous supper. After lunch, as the weather had cleared, we set forth. [1]

We had no clear and accurate line of march, mainly because the map was useless except for giving the general trend of the country. We went through the village and came out onto a side road, along which we trudged in the general direction of the hills. Progress was slowed by the conversations we were continually compelled to make with passing Italians. It came out in the end that we were usually taken for returning Italian soldiers, of whom there were many thousands roaming the countryside. The locals were very anxious to get news of those they knew.

Because of these delays, by the time darkness began to fall we had only covered half a dozen odd miles to reach the tiny village of La Trinità, a mere handful of houses in a sparsely inhabited valley. We found the villagers very friendly and ready to help, but as they were very poor and the houses small, we were split between two families for the evening meal. We gathered afterwards to hear the wireless news.

The big item for the day was the BBC announcement regarding ex-prisoners in Italy. The Germans had said they would shoot all those who did not give themselves up within a time limit, if they were recaptured. The enemy was officially warned that if this threat were carried out, those responsible would pay the full penalty. They were told that if they did succeed in recapturing ex-prisoners, they must treat them according to the Geneva Convention.

The following morning, 2 October, dawned fine and sunny after the dull afternoon of the previous day. After a hearty farewell from the village, we set off up a steep mule track through the chestnut forest for the village of Rigollo in the adjoining valley. Quickly we gained altitude and after a strenuous hour of climbing we breasted the ridge to be rewarded with a glorious view. Mountain and valley tangled together into the blue distance beneath the cloudless Italian sky.

John Langrishe recalled their routine:

There was always the problem, towards the end of a day's march, of finding lodgings for the night in a village, because there was the ever-present possibility of some unfriendly Italian being tempted to give us away to the Germans. One way which logically seemed 'safe' was to buttonhole someone working in the fields outside the chosen village, since it was unlikely that anyone performing such menial but important work would be on the side of the oppressors, and indeed these simple precautions never really let us down.

After two exhausting days, the escapers were greeted on the outskirts of the hilltop village of Pieve di Bardi by a stocky, weather-beaten man leading a bullock hitched to a wooden sledge. He said: 'Good evening boys, what can I do for you?' in perfect Cockney, and introduced himself as Agostino Ferrari. He had been chef for 22 years in the Connaught Rooms in Long Acre in Holborn, London.

Signor Ferrari arranged for them to receive food and lodging from some of the 20 families in the village. The officers were accommodated in a hayloft and then in a stone hut left vacant by another quartet from Fontanellato who left to make their way south.

John Langrishe recalled:

While staying in Pieve we encountered another strange facet of wartime in Italy. One evening, Agostino said he would take us to hear the news in English, so after supper we set forth in the pitch darkness, stumbling along behind him over the rough forest paths for about quarter of an hour.

We came upon a wooden cabin in the clearing and Agostino knocked on the door. We were led up the stairs into a crowded, smoky room where several Italians were bunched around a magnificent and obviously very expensive radio. The contrast between the luxury of this electrical equipment and the rude dwelling which contained it was striking. This was the first of several we encountered, but I never solved the mystery of the radiograms in the log cabins to my satisfaction.

By 9 October, John and Bunny had come to the decision that they wanted to set out on their own way south into Tuscany. They had heard that the cooking in that region was the best in Italy. However, they could not leave on that day as from dawn till dusk the heavens wept solid water. Furthermore, we were forced to spend a cold, cheerless afternoon concealed in our loft when two Fascist policemen put in an appearance. Agostino was very worried as he feared he might have been given away by the priest in the next village, who was ardently anti-Ally, but all the Fascists were looking for were secret hoards of potatoes that ought to have been sent to Germany. As soon as they had gone, we sallied forth to warm over Agostino's fire and talk of the days before the war.

The next day, John and Bunny made their departure. It was sad to see them go. But as Buck was grounded temporarily by his feet, I could not accompany them and leave him on his own. Further, we had intended to make for Ancona in the hope of finding some naval escape organisation there, but the other two favoured Tuscany, as has already been said.

I heard no more of them for many months and then it was sad news. They did indeed reach their chosen Tuscany, but were picked up by the Germans and taken off to Germany.

Captain Buchanan and Lieutenant Langrishe stayed at Pieve di Bardi until 19 October. They crystallised a new plan:

First we would make a wide circle round the nearby town of Borgotaro, where there was a sizeable German force and local HQ, and then make our way along the line of the mountains, keeping as far as possible in the hills and working our way southwards.

We abandoned our idea of making for Ancona. We decided that a long walk with the fighting chance of ultimate success was preferable to the lottery of a way out by sea - even though we had received rumours of some official organisation to that end.

We considered that if we avoided any village of more than a dozen houses, stayed off main roads and kept moving, common sense and our general army training would help us through. The problem of how to get across the German lines was shelved until such time as the question became more immediate.

After a month the pair crossed the Apennines. They had already travelled 330 kilometres. The route then lay into the Arno and Tiber valleys, south-east to Perugia, and finally into the Abruzzo and on to the front line, where most escapes came to grief. On 8 November the officers reached the hamlet of Tripozzo in the Commune of Arrone in Umbria. A local partisan persuaded them to take another fugitive with them, a bedraggled Spaniard who had served for 10 years in the French Foreign Legion. His name was Sebastian.

John Langrishe recalled:

As light was beginning to fail, we spotted a small village below. Neither of us liked the look of it, but there was no other in sight, so we went down to try to find lodging there. It was a poor little place by the name of Fano. We found a house to take us in and were soon sitting warming the chill from our bones before a huge fire. Time wore on and I was beginning to get concerned about our meal as there were no signs of anything cooking in the two-roomed house. Later, the owner came in. He was a poor peasant, and putting some chestnuts in a sort of wire cage, held them over the fire to roast.

This was our meal, about two pounds of roast chestnuts apiece, so it was just as well that we had been able to find a good lunch en route. Our host showed us to the bedroom, a small, very draughty barn with only a few wisps of straw each - no blankets. Lying there in the cold, Buck and I had another of our conferences. He was feeling rather depressed because he felt that his feet were beginning to give out and looking ruefully at them said: 'Blast you, my two worst enemies.'

From the latest war news, we gathered that the line was still somewhere near the Sangro River. At the present rate of progress, we might hope to be on the right side of the war in about a week. We were also coming into the forward areas, where we expected to find more Germans. So we reconsidered our plans.

We reasoned that if we should find ourselves in a tight corner, one might get away, whereas two or three would merely attract unwelcome attention. Further, we thought that the nearer we were to the fighting zone, the harder it would be to find accommodation, and came reluctantly to the conclusion that we should part on the morrow and make our separate ways.

It was arranged that after breakfast, if any, we would draw lots for the starting order and depart at 15-minute intervals. We exchanged addresses to carry news to our families. This done, we fell into a cold and uneasy slumber.

There was a breakfast next morning, but only just. As a change from the evening, we had boiled chestnuts. Any youthful enthusiasm I might have had for these nuts was by then effectively killed. A few nicely roast after a good dinner on a winter's evening are all very well, but to have to start the day (and a grey one at that) on a plateful of luke warm, soggy nuts was nothing to write to Mrs Beeton about.

Buck, Sebastian and I drew lots for the starting order. It fell to me to go first, followed by Buck, with the Spaniard bringing up the rear. As I prepared to leave, I could not help a feeling of sadness at this parting, but knew that we must not change our plans once they had been decided. Buck and I had walked together for 400 miles and it was 42 days since we left Toccalmatto. We had grown to know each other very well, including those little faults and idiosyncrasies which go to make up each individual. We may have had our small differences, but on the whole those 42 days are ones that I could look back on and say: 'I had a good friend with me.'

Chatting with our host at breakfast over cups of tea (yes, tea!), he told of a very interesting occurrence in the valley which had aroused the intense admiration of the Italians for the English...

There had been a party of about two dozen RAF officers and men who had escaped in the same way as ourselves from a small camp not far away. They had begun to walk to the lines, but as they had been trained to aerial and not ground navigation, they decided they could go no further. Or perhaps they found walking slow after flying.

They settled down in a village nearby and thought things out carefully. It was an isolated settlement on the top of a hill with a little plateau. A small party then volunteered to make their way across the lines and come back for the rest in an aeroplane at the next full moon, then about a fortnight distant. Those who were left behind had to prepare a landing ground with the help of the villagers, who caught on to the plan with enthusiasm, though they did not really think the 'English Air Force' would be able to do what was planned.

All got more excited until at last the great day came. The night was fine and clear, the fires were lit, and all the villagers and the airmen waited at the edge of the plateau, wondering whether the longed-for aeroplane would come. Had their friends got through or been recaptured by the Germans?

Time passed and the brilliance of an Italian moon flooded the countryside and picked out the white walls of the houses at the back of the plateau. Suddenly the distant hum of engines was heard, the sound grew and soon it became a full-throated roar overhead. The motors were cut and in a few more moments bouncing along over the uneven turf was a Wellington bomber. It came to rest, swung round, and in a rush the ground party was swept within its doors. A final word of thanks to the Italians and perhaps a carton of cigarettes thrown out, then, with a roar from the engines, the pilot swung the aircraft into the centre of the runway and it was gone into the night, leaving only a smell of oil and a crowd of thunderstruck Italians.

Such was the story he told, finishing by suggesting that we ought to have arranged something similar for ourselves.

Buck and I shook hands, wished each other luck, and then I launched off on my own. He stayed put and was liberated when the Allies finally reached the area in 1944.

As I came to the main road, peeping cautiously first one way and then the other, two Germans were to be seen lounging at the gate of a large house some 50 yards up the road. I waited for a minute till they were looking the other way, then stepped smartly across the road and down a lane.

Walking speedily for a quarter of an hour to put the village well behind, I came to a good farm road where there was a labourer trimming the ditches. I told him who I was and asked which of the two roads I could see just ahead was the right one for the village of Pizzoli. He replied that quite a few ex-prisoners had passed and that they had always taken the right fork, not the one to Pizzoli.

It had been my invariable rule never to accept the advice of any Italian for two reasons. Firstly, they might have given directions to send one into enemy hands, and secondly, as they really had no idea of what we were up against, their advice, though honestly given, was usually inapplicable to our circumstances. But on this occasion, whether through some sixth sense or because I was feeling very much alone, I decided to accept, thereby setting in motion a chain of circumstances the outcome of which was very satisfactory from my point of view.

If I had turned to the left, I should have probably put my head into the hornet's nest of Aquila. Some sort of Providence turned my feet to the hills again and in the hills there were always ready helpers among the Italians.

In the village of Casamaina in the Abruzzo an Italian helper called Mario told John Langrishe another strange tale:

It seemed that not long before I came there, one evening when all windows and doors were securely shuttered and barred against the night, there came the sound of marching feet from the road where it curled round against the head of the valley before entering the village. All immediately feared the worse. The Germans were coming to search the village, and their fears were not at all allayed when, as the marching footsteps came into the village, a deep voice shouted 'Halt!'

Mario said that the men had stopped outside his house. He peeped through the curtains to see about 30 troops drawn up in formation with tommy guns slung across their shoulders. What was worse, they were wearing the round parachutists' helmets. In a moment there was a knock on the door. He opened it with some misgivings, to find a tall man standing outside in full equipment and heavily armed, the firelight glinting on the metal. Mario wondered what his fate was to be when, to his utter surprise, the man addressed him in Italian, saying that he was the commander of a platoon of South African paratroops and wanted lodging for his men for the night.

This was soon arranged as Mario was the headman of the village. Finding they were not the hated Germans was a great relief to everyone in the tiny settlement, who were happy to welcome these men from such distant parts.

The parachutists were parcelled out in twos and threes around the various houses, the officer remaining with Mario. He assured him that he and his men would be gone before dawn. He said that they had been dropped near Terni with maps and compasses for escaping prisoners and had also carried out a demolition near there. They had been marching through enemy-occupied territory and would split up into small groups when they were nearer the fighting line. They were as good as their word. When the villagers began to stir next morning, they did indeed find their overnight guests had departed at a very early hour.

The whole affair had caught the imagination of the locals, Italians always being fond of anything in the cloak and dagger line anyway, and a great deal of good propaganda had resulted from this incident.

On 14 November John Langrishe was excited by the prospect of being among friends again in perhaps three or four days. So he decided to press on despite bad weather and lack of protective clothing:

There was a track leading out of the village of Secinaro, under the side of Monte Sirente, a height of around 7,000 feet, which afforded some slight shelter from the strong wind. The way led up gently for a couple of miles then suddenly came out on to a high, exposed plateau across which the rain and wind lashed mercilessly. My clothes were all ringing wet in no time at all. But I was getting near to the end of my journey. Excitement was rising as the realisation of all my hopes came nearer. Peering ahead through the mist and low cloud, I fancied I could see mountains which would be in Allied hands. Probably this was fallacious, but it gave me great encouragement to think that beyond those rain-washed hills was the British Eighth Army.

Only 40 miles or so away they were. I must not fall into the hands of the Germans at this stage and I thought of the amusement it would cause if they had caught me after travelling hundreds of miles. I determined to proceed with redoubled care and common sense.

Sodden clothes and an empty stomach meant nothing now as I pressed on at my best speed over the barren moor, my only companions a flock of goats with a small, ragged urchin in attendance.

Ahead lay a cauldron of mountain, cloud and rain, with a heavy grey sky over all:

Three hundred feet above me, perched on a rocky crag, was Castrovalva, like a fairy tale village. But it seemed a long way off at the end of the day, tired as I was and wet through, with the sodden clothing chaffing my skin at every step. But I must climb the hill to the village or stay wet in the open for the night.

With each yard of the steep path my willpower began to flag. A voice inside me seemed to say: 'Sit down and rest awhile.' But I knew that should I do this, I would feel far more tired when I rose to go on. I had eaten nothing but a couple of crusts since breakfast and it was then after five. I had walked about 18 miles of really mountainous country in rain and sleet. In short, I was just about all in.

Somehow, as dusk was falling, I found myself on the mountain road leading down into Castrovalva from the back of the village. When I came to the first house, I knocked to ask for shelter. I could not have gone to the next had I been refused. I was so exhausted.

In a moment the door was opened by a bent old woman who bade me enter without further ado. When I told her that I was an English officer, she said she would do all that she could for me, and showed messages left by previous travellers telling of her kindness. Some happened to be friends of mine. There was a good fire roaring in the chimney and I am afraid that I made straight for this and stood in front, my clothes steaming furiously, while Maria Divito, as her name was, went to prepare some hot food.

Sitting over my meal, I told her briefly about my travels and how excited I was that I was finally on the last stage of my trip. She said that the fighting was only on the other side of the mountains, about 15 miles in a direct line. Maria added that many English had come through the village and that all the Italians were anxious to do everything they could do to help, though, and this said with a sly grin, some were more helpful than others. I asked if she knew anyone who could give me some information as to the best route to be followed for the last stage. Maria told me that a man was coming to see her soon who might be able to assist.

It occurred to me that as there was a perfectly good road up from Aversa which cars could use, even though it was steep, that Germans might be in the habit of paying unwelcome visits. But Maria assured me that it was quite all right. They seldom came, she said, and when they did there was always ample warning from the roaring of the motors or from a phone call in good time from friends below.

As we were sitting before the fire after supper, there was a knock on the door, which opened to admit a large, florid Italian. He was the visitor Maria had referred to earlier on, and gave me a great deal of useful information. Firstly, he said that the German line ran through Alfedena and Castel di Sangro and that it was believed to be lightly held; secondly that there were several other English people in the village waiting for a good break in the weather; and thirdly, that an Italian guide was due to return from the Allied line to take another party over. This was thrilling news indeed and I said I would make contact in the morning.

Next day, John Langrishe met an RAF sergeant pilot called Bill, together with the Italian guide who had just returned from crossing the lines. He was eager to repeat the trip, but warned that the weather was deteriorating.

In the afternoon on the following day, two comrades from Fontanellato walked in. Lieutenant Nigel Knight-Bruce and his friend Archie had followed roughly the same route from Fontanellato, but four days in advance of the others. They had already made one failed attempt to cross the lines. The pair also joined the expedition.

Ahead lay the highest mountains, snow and ice, and the Germans along the Gustav Line, the winter defensive position. The Allies had also just decided to launch an offensive.

NOTES

[1] I have discovered that the farmer in Vigoleno who welcomed the escapers for the first overnight stop was Signor Alberto Sanini. A note left with him by Captain Buchanan reads: 'This is to certify that the bearer of this note has provided one day's food and lodging to four British officers.'

3 The German Lines

The Allied escapers and evaders assembled in the little village of Castrovalva at nine in the morning on 17 November 1943. There were about 20 servicemen in total, Britons, South Africans and Americans. To their dismay, there were also 60 or more Italian civilians. Most were carrying ancient suitcases lashed up with cords and string. The men split into parties of five or six and set off through the pinewoods into the mountains. The Italians were at the head of the winding column.

The first night stop was the abandoned village of San Lorenzo, which is about half way. In the morning, the order of march was reversed, with the Allied contingent taking the lead. Soon they entered a snowfield. A game warden in a lonely hut told the fugitives that the main danger was from German ski patrols.

John Langrishe recalled:

> Away we trudged in the snow, following the guide like a snake over the brow of a ridge, when we saw the whole of the upper valley laid out before us clad in shimmering white. There was no sign of life apart from a hut in the middle distance, its dark brown form breaking the landscape. Occasionally we met old ski tracks, but for the most part the sparkling sheen of the snow was unmarked and reflected the bright sun with a million dancing facets of light, so that I had to screw up my eyes against the glare.
>
> The snow being two foot deep and more, it often spilled over the tops of my boots and I was soon walking with a pool of water inside them, and the bottoms of my trousers were encrusted with ice. I could see the column winding across the snowfield, but some of the Italians were making very heavy weather and finding that their bulging suitcases were hardly worth the labour. In contrast, the Allied contingent were travelling well. Suddenly, I heard the sound of aeroplane engines above the crunch of boots and the moan of the wind.
>
> A small formation of fighters, the red, white and blue roundels on their wings catching the sun, swept over the snow-clad peak and across the valley, banking this way and that as they kept their watch for Germans. It was a great moment to see our friends so near, but the thought struck me that we might be mistaken for a German column. At that height and speed the planes could not

possibly tell whether we were friend or foe and the fact that we had adopted a military formation might have attracted more attention than we desired. But we were in luck, for with a final swoop the aircraft banked away out of sight over the ridge and were gone.

Slowly, slowly, we ate up the distance to the hut, making our way around the edge of a frozen lake until we reached the sanctuary. Though there was neither fire nor anyone living there, it seemed very warm after the snows outside. So all crowded in, stamping their feet to shake off the snow and dumping their loads on the floor to ease their arms and shoulders. Eager hands unpacked food from pockets and haversacks and shared it with those who were without. The mutual warmth created by so many bodies within the confined space helped to thaw out those who were cold and loosened tongues until the room seemed on the way to rivalling the Tower of Babel.

In half an hour appetites had been satisfied and thirsts quenched from the well water. The guide made signs that he wanted to continue. Archie, Bill and I had a word with him to try to get some idea of what was coming. He explained that when we got over the next crest the path led down all the way and we should be able to see the Allied-held country laid out before us. The guide added that he hoped to be able to get through by his usual route, which the warden had confirmed was still open when asked about it earlier in the morning. We held a council of war amongst ourselves and passed round instructions that groups should not exceed six in number and that there must be at least 50 metres between each. If the head ran into trouble, those further from the storm centre would have a better chance of escape.

The Italians did not take kindly to this minor example of discipline, but they eventually agreed to do as we told them. So there was a general upheaval as loads were taken up and groups marshalled by their leaders. The guide moved towards the door and in a moment we were out again in the sun and snow. He led us along the foot of Monte Greco, towering more than a thousand feet above on our right, past the lake and towards a ridge. As we toiled up the steep slope the snow became deeper, first half way up our calves, then to our knees, and finally we were thrusting through thigh-deep drifts. It was agonisingly slow going and I sensed the precious daylight slipping away as we all wallowed among the whiteness, ever struggling upwards.

But the hard going had one good result for, if the Italians tended to bunch together on the level, the slope opened them out as the less physically fit among them laboured up with their bags and cases. As we approached the summit, the wind began to sweep down over the ridge with ever-increasing velocity. Its chill breath cut through my damp clothing like a sharp knife, making me shiver even though I was sweating profusely from exertions of the climb. The depth of the drifted snow lessened until, when we at last reached the top, we were walking on bare black rock, the snow only lying in nooks and crannies where it had escaped the sweeping action of the wind.

I felt a great thrill go through me as, after months of wandering and hundreds of miles, I at last looked down on to country where there were Allied troops. It was an indescribable sensation to stand where we did on the summit of this range, amid the snows, and look down on a vast expanse of dark green country, knowing that over there lay the end of our journey. We were on the very last lap and I confess that I uttered a silent prayer for safe going over the final few miles. We knew that the enemy was entrenched right below us. Just where, we should soon find out.

The column stopped for some 10 minutes beneath a small group of storm-bent trees while the guide went on ahead to scout the lie of the land. I swept the country with my eyes for any signs of life, but there were none. The guide returned, indicating that it was safe to proceed, so once more the column came to life.

As we descended in single file, the trees became denser and we were soon marching down a very narrow, rough and steep defile into a forest. Silence was ordered, but it was almost impossible to clamber down among the rocks and boulders without an accompanying crash of stones and an occasional oath as a shin was torn on an outcrop of rock. Down and down we went, turning, twisting and tumbling over and among the boulders until the guide signed to us to stop while he went ahead again.

He was gone 10 minutes and when he returned his face was long and he looked depressed and worried. He explained that a hundred yards on he had come round a corner to find a party of Germans cutting wood and blocking the route. There was another pathway further to the east which he would try.

I asked what we should do, as the column was in single file with the Allied contingent in front. For us to double back on ourselves would be a most complicated manoeuvre through the very narrow path. The guide said that it would better for him alone to clamber back and for the tail end of the column to become the front. Both Bill and I received this idea with considerable apprehension since it would mean that the Allied section would be at the back, but we realised the impossibility of doing anything else. In the events that followed, it turned out to have been the best for us.

The guide left us and made his way slowly and with difficulty past the length of the column, through the stones and boulders up the narrow path. We sat down again to wait until the time came to move on. We conversed in quiet undertones for we could hear the ringing of the axes on the trees below and occasionally the crash of falling timber as the Germans gathered their firewood.

Ten minutes passed, then half an hour, and still no signs of movement in the column. So we decided to copy the example of the guide and go back on our tracks. With difficulty we made our way up to the top of the gorge, telling the Italians to follow in due course. We found that the men at the end had failed to accompany the guide, who had gone on by himself, saying that they had been afraid. Bill and I were livid for we were now without anyone who knew the lie of the land. There was nothing to do but take the lead ourselves.

When we first arrived at the head of the gorge after crossing the snowfield, we met a couple of British lieutenant colonels returning after an unsuccessful attempt to get through. They told us that the place was swarming with enemy and that any attempt under the present circumstances was doomed to failure. When they saw the numbers in our column they nearly threw a fit on the spot. I felt afterwards that for senior officers their attempt must have been singularly half-hearted and that their advice, well meaning though it was, might have deterred us from our own try. Incidentally, they got through successfully the night after we saw them.

As we passed the last of the Italians, we saw some telephone cables on the ground and sent back word to avoid disturbing them at all costs. We were in a small wood and while we discussed our next move, we heard guns firing only a hundred yards or so from us. I surmised that the wires we had seen were linked to an observer who was probably on the hill to our left. If the cables were cut, as some suggested, a party would be sent out immediately to find the break and we would be discovered.

We walked slowly and silently through the trees and soon came to the end of the wood. An excellent view could be had of the front. Again we halted to confer. My view was that two or three had better go forward to the edge of the hill before dusk and try to see where the Allied line lay. Archie, Nigel with his glasses, Bill and I, went forward after sending the rest of the party back under cover of the wood with strict orders to observe silence, explaining that our success depended on not arousing the suspicions of the Germans, now so close to us.

Creeping to the edge of the hill, we lay down and made a thorough examination of the ground in front with the aid of Nigel's field glasses, though none of us had the vaguest idea where the German positions ended or the Allied lines began. At the foot of the mountain ran the Sangro River across our front. On the right lay the tiny village of Alfedena with flames licking round the houses. Further to our right we could just make out, some four or five miles away, the town of Castel di Sangro, also fired by the Germans and burning merrily.

Immediately below and only a hundred yards away were the snouts of two 88mm German guns projecting from their pits dug into the side of the hill. Beyond the river the country was undulating, dark green with a white ribbon of a road running diagonally across from Castel di Sangro into the distance. Every now and then there would be the grey burst of an Allied shell in the middle distance, but still no indication of the demarcation between friend and foe. Suddenly we were shaken by the thump of firing from the guns beneath our feet. As an artillery officer, from sheer force of habit, I grabbed the glasses to spot the fall of the shot.

The first round I missed, but heard the dull clang of its detonation to the left front. When they fired again, I spotted the white puff of the shell burst on the crest of a range of hills which ran along the horizon to our left, some six or seven miles away. Thereafter it was easy, for each round of the dozen or so fired was on that ridge, but each a little to the right of its predecessor, telling me all that I wanted to know. I must have given a little grunt of satisfaction for Archie asked me whether I had seen anything of interest. I replied that the shelling was obviously the

Germans ranging on the forward line of Allied troops. If we could reach those hills, I was confident that we would be safe.

I called the senior members of each of the Allied parties and the eldest and most sensible looking of the Italians in order to make a plan. When they came up their first question was whether we had been able to see anything and if I knew where the enemy was. We again all lay on our faces on the grass and the plan was formulated.

I said that there was German artillery between us and the river and there might also be infantry on the other bank, but added that the line of hills in the distance was almost certainly in Allied hands. Then came the question of what to do. I said that each party of no more than six should form up on the crest, but with a lateral distance of at least two hundred yards between each. When it was dark, each group should set forth down the hill towards the river and be quite independent. I told the Italians to form up and go left along the hillside for at least two thousand metres, through a tree-clad height and then down to the river, at the same time urging on them absolute silence. No one was to leave the shelter of the wood till it was dark. Then, wishing them all good luck, we split up into our various groups.

My little party assembled and sat down on the grass to wait for darkness. It consisted of Bill and two American airmen, Archie, Nigel and myself. We discussed our plan of march, deciding to take it in turn to lead. Bill and the Americans, being airmen, had little idea of what to do, but it was impressed on them that once we were on the way it was imperative to keep utter silence. Darkness fell in a few minutes and I began to be concerned as to how we were going to be able to keep our line of march directed on the hills. The burning houses on each flank would be a help. Stars there were none, as the sky was overcast with heavy clouds.

The very last section of our journey was about to commence and I for one rose to my feet with a thrill in my heart. The final thing to do before setting off was to decide the first leader. After some argument, I found myself in this somewhat unenviable position on the apparent grounds that I knew more than the others. I must, however, admit that in one way I was glad, for I would only have myself to blame if the party walked into the enemy. But it was a heavy responsibility to bear.

I gave the word to move in single file down the hill. Slowly, step by step, we descended, directing our way between the two gun emplacements which I had seen from the top of the hill. All was silent until suddenly I heard a telephone bell ring almost beneath my feet. I froze in my tracks and whispered to Archie to pass the word back to turn round and go up the hill. Silently we retraced our steps for 50 feet and then halted to make a new plan. We had walked almost on top of the enemy command post, but by great good fortune had not been heard.

Through the quiet of the night there then came to us the sound of distant voices and the crash of people making their way through the woods away to our left. It was the Italians observing their rule of silence like a herd of elephants in the jungle. In another moment we heard a German voice roar *'Alt'* and again *'Alt'* followed a few seconds later by a burst of machine gun fire and then another. We all wondered what was happening to those poor devils with their suitcases and bags, but realised that for us it was the best thing that could have happened for it drew off the Germans to that side.

Calling my group to their feet, we set off again down the hillside, but this time we went further to our right before going down in order to be clear of the guns. As before, we slowly and carefully picked our way over the turf until we came to a stone wall, over which we climbed successfully in silence. We crept along the line of the wall which turned down the hill, on and on, down and down. Still no sign of a German anywhere except for the shouting on our left some hundreds of yards away. Then the rain began to fall, at first lightly, but heavily in a few minutes, another great aid to our adventure.

Over another wall and through some brambles and we found ourselves on a railway line by a viaduct which had been blown-up. The river was close now, just the other side of a road, and I could see the foaming water gleaming softly through the darkness. I wondered where we were going to find the forward German infantry and their barbed wire and mines. It was heart-stopping work, creeping silently forward through the midst of our enemies.

Thinking it dangerous to clamber over the railway line, I led my party down a small torrent which ran beneath the viaduct, over the road and across a bushy common to the edge of the Sangro River. We were dismayed when we saw that it was some 30 yards wide with the water boiling and foaming between its banks. Had there been a bridge we could not possibly have used it. There was no alternative but to wade or swim to the other side. One of the party found a long pole and volunteered to lead us over. We formed a human chain by linking hands and in we went. It was icy cold and the force of the current tore at our feet and bodies, trying to wrench us off our balance and plunge us all into the stream. But we held firm and foot by foot forced our way slowly to the other side. We emerged dripping and out of breath, the water having been to the level of our waists.

The riverbank was no place to dally, so once more I set off across the fields. It was very difficult to keep in the right direction and I asked the others quietly if any by chance had a compass. One of the Americans produced a stud with a tiny compass in the end of it, a child's toy almost but on this occasion worth its weight in gold. It had been issued to him as escape apparatus. We were still in the dark, but all of a sudden a tremendous battle began over on our right near Isernia. By the light, I caught a glimpse of the hills ahead and was able to take a rapid compass bearing.

Before going on I said that I would stop every two or three minutes, when all would strain their ears for any sound. Forward we went, the silence only broken by the squelch of boots in the soft grass, over one meadow, then another, then stop to listen, but there was not a sound. Behind on our right glowed the burning village of Alfedena. On the left we could see the flames licking through the houses of Castel di Sangro and far away to the right was the battle near Isernia. It was an amazing sight from where we were, the glow of shell bursts with the coloured tracer bouncing up and down the mountainside. But all that fell round us was the drenching rain, steadily and remorselessly, whilst overhead there whistled the occasional shell from British guns on their way to burst against the mountains we had left.

I came to a road and a damaged railway beside it and the village cemetery of Alfedena, but thankfully still no sign of a German. We crossed small streams and another road then took to the fields again, moving as fast as caution and the need for silence would permit. Still our occasional stops revealed no sounds in the night. We had been going for five hours or more when we came to a ruined and deserted farm. Having made certain that it was occupied by neither side, the six of us sat down in the shelter of a shed and ate what we had left of our food, consisting of bread and jam.

It was a welcome halt for we had been marching for about 18 hours almost continuously. The food did us good and we talked over what had occurred, giving us a certain feeling of achievement. I was coming to the belief that we were probably through the main German defences, if any such existed, as we were then some five miles beyond the guns. From experience I knew that field artillery was usually closer than that to its infantry. But there was still the danger of running into patrols, both enemy or our own, who would fire at anything moving through the night if we bumped into them. But we must be on the move again for our clothes were sodden from the rain and the river and would soon have made us chilled through. So having eaten the last of our food, we got to our feet once more.

Over deserted stubble, through brambles and hedges, we came to the road we had seen from the top of the hill running from Castel di Sangro to the south. Beyond this we could see a wide plain with many dark objects scattered about, which later turned out to be wandering cattle. In the middle of this plain we came upon a small stream which was too wide to jump, so it meant another wade, though it mattered not to our boots already utterly soaked from the Sangro crossing.

In half an hour we were on the other side of the plain at the foot of the range of hills on which the German guns had been firing earlier in the evening. I looked about for a path leading upwards but found none, only a gap in the brush which clothed the slopes of the hills, so started the climb from there. The rain began to fall more heavily still after having eased off somewhat for the last couple of hours. To make matters worse, when we were all in the middle of a deep thicket Bill called out that his shoes had completely collapsed and dropped to pieces. All I could do to help was to give him the three pairs of spare socks I had been carrying, all of which he put on in place of shoes. It was terrible going as we fought our way upwards. It was impossible to move silently through the dense undergrowth as we slipped and fell, scrambled and thrust our way forward yard by yard, pulling and pushing Bill alternately when his stockinged feet slid on the greasy ground.

The rain poured from the black sky and the battle, now behind us, raged, with the tracer still bouncing on the hillsides for all the world like a great neon sign gone mad. The six of us tired, soaked and hungry men dragged our limbs up the hill to safety. After two hours of struggle, the brush opened out and fell behind us and we found ourselves in open country again near the crest of the ridge. With the vanquishing of one difficulty, another came upon us. The temperature rapidly dropped many degrees and we all shivered violently after the exertions of the climb. On and on till the ground before us levelled out and the first grey light of dawn crept over the hills in front of us.

In a little while we came to a rough track running between low hedges on which I noticed cables resting. Eagerly we took them in our hands to see whether they were German and came to the conclusion, both from the way they were laid and the type, that they could only be British - a tremendous moment in a day of great events. Their general direction was away from the ridge which we had just surmounted, so I decided to follow them. But after a mile we lost the wires in broken country in the half-light of dawn.

Gradually the light strengthened to show us that we were once more on high ground, broken and criss-crossed by gullies and hummocks but quite bare of any sign of life or habitation. We wearily dragged our tortured feet along. All were tired beyond words for we had now been going steadily for 24 hours over some of the worst country in Italy, though my long walk had toughened me for this final effort.

For another hour we all struggled slowly onwards until, with the red flush of the true dawn rising over the mountains, we came to the edge of our plateau and met another track leading down into the dark valley below. There was no sign of life yet and we almost wondered whether we had penetrated to the lost world, for there was nothing moving and no sound anywhere. Even the battle behind us was silent at last. We halted for a rest, but when I suggested that we go on, four of the party said they had had enough and would wait till they were picked up by Allied troops. So I went on with one of the American airmen down the track.

We trudged on like automatons, but fortunately the way now was all down hill, the track improving all the while and the light gradually flooding over the valley. Another hour, during which we hardly exchanged a word, then we came round a bend to meet an old peasant driving two cows to pasture, and saw a small village a mile or so further on down the track. I bade the old man good morning and tried my usual opening gambit of 'Are there Germans in the village?' And now for the greatest moment of the past three months when he replied: 'No, there are no Germans. The Americans are here.'

The American and I looked at each other silently. We were through. Our efforts had been crowned with success and our trials and tribulations had not been in vain. As these and other thoughts flashed through our heads, we began to run in our excited haste to speak to our own people again, the fatigue for the moment being banished by the thrill of success. Our wearied and long suffering feet seemed to have wings as we clattered down over the cobble stones into the village of Cerro.

At the first house on the left as we entered, we saw some American troops washing and cooking in the garden. We stopped long enough to ask where the local headquarters was and to collect some cigarettes, then we were away again. In the centre of the village we enquired of an Italian where the commander was and he pointed out a house further down the street. As we hammered on the door, I asked my friend to do the talking, as these were his own folk.

The door opened and a head with a sleepy pair of eyes looked out. 'We are escaped prisoners,' my friend said. 'Oh yeah,' said the head, glancing at our battered clothes, and slamming the door. Catching each other's eyes, we laughed and knocked again. When the door opened, my friend said: 'Say, I'm an American officer and my friend here is English.' This time the head smiled and said: 'Sorry, I took you for Italians. Come right on in.'

Inside the house was all stir and bustle with men shaving, dressing, and preparing breakfast. Our welcome was as warm as the first attempt had been frigid. In a moment we were sitting down at a table with mugs of steaming coffee and piled plates before us, which we steadily consumed, all the while answering a thousand questions from the eager GIs. Soon there was a shout of 'What's a goin' on in here?' and a major entered the room. He was told that we were a couple of escapees and, as we had nearly finished our meal, asked us into his office and gave us another hearty welcome and congratulations. Over the remains of our coffee and a cigarette, we answered the many questions he put about our route and the German troops through whose lines we had come. On his map we showed him the lie of the land.

The major then explained that his was a battalion of airborne troops operating as infantry on the left of the Eighth Army and forming the link with the Fifth Army. He then asked me whether I wished to be repatriated through the Eighth or Fifth, to which I replied the former as I thought my own regiment might be with them.

The escapers found a British Royal Engineers captain who was preparing for the arrival of his brigade HQ. Archie and Nigel drifted in later. A scout car had just arrived to take them all to Divisional HQ in Cantalupo when Bill also turned up, footsore but rebooted. From that village they were carried by lorry to Campobasso and Corps HQ, together with other escapers. The servicemen were given new clothing, fed, interviewed by Intelligence Staff, and sent on to Lucera and Foggia.

John Langrishe recalled journey's end:

Bari, Taranto and Bizerta were the next stages. From there to Algiers by rail, a musical comedy journey, and air to Prestwick via Marrakesh, were the last stages. My front door in Edinburgh opened to receive me at 7.15pm on 23 December 1943. I had jokingly said that I wanted to be home by Christmas, though I never dreamed in my wildest moments that my intention would be uncannily fulfilled.

After many weeks leave - extra rations, petrol, etc. - I was posted back to my regiment, then in Felixstowe. We landed in France on D-Day plus four in June 1944, and I went with them to the very end of the war. I was demobbed in August 1946 and returned to my pre-war job, qualifying as a solicitor. [1]

John Langrishe's long walk out from Fontanellato to the Sangro took seven weeks and a day and he travelled 530 miles in 34 stages. He was Mentioned in Despatches for his actions.

NOTES

[1] The Official War History states:

The infantry of the 17th Brigade advanced from ridge to ridge, the artillery engaged German batteries in the farther hills, and on the night of 22 November our patrols entered Alfedena and found no Germans there.

John Langrishe recalled: 'I had passed by Alfedena on the night of 19 November.'

4 Ticket to Como

Italian writer Renata Broggini described the wartime Italo-Swiss border as 'the frontier of hope.' The Alpine passes saw a constant flow of political and Jewish fugitives, industrialists and workers, mothers and children, priests, writers, partisans - and Allied escapers and evaders.

Though service escapers were free men under International Law, they were subject to a measure of military control as the result of an agreement between the British and Swiss governments. The men were confined in the north-eastern cantons. Officers were given an allowance and found their own food and lodging. 'Other ranks' were billeted in empty buildings such as factories and schools. From January 1944 the servicemen were allowed to volunteer for work in agriculture, forestry and land drainage. They lived on farms or in purpose-built barracks. The number of Allied personnel eventually rose to 5,143. The liberation of southern France in August 1944 by the 7th Army opened a land corridor and allowed the repatriation of all the men by the end of the year.

This is the story of one of the English escapers who took the most direct route to Switzerland: a journey by rail, a lake crossing and a mountain trek. George Almond was born in Blackpool, but spent most of his pre-war years in Blackburn. The 22-year-old lance corporal was a draughtsman (architectural) in the Engineers Services section of the Royal Engineers. He served in Palestine and Syria and was captured by the Germans at Mersa Matruh in north-western Egypt on 29 June 1942. On 20 September George Almond's commanding officer, Captain Bernard Jarvis, wrote from Middle East Forces to his mother and father:

> Last week I heard from Corps HQ that it had been confirmed that Lance Corporal GC Almond was missing. I think that I can tell you better than anyone how it came about.
>
> Almond was one of the draughtsmen in my office staff and we all moved together quite suddenly to the desert. We arrived when things were at their worst. When it became clear that we were in for a running battle, I was ordered to cut the staff to a minimum. The Chief Clerk selected his assistant, Lance Corporal Miller from Glasgow, and I stipulated that Almond should be the draughtsman. The remainder were sent back to the base area.
>
> The battle was very much one-sided at that time, and by a piece of bad luck we found ourselves cut off with no means of

supply. We waited during the whole of one day, it was Sunday, 29 June, in order to break out during the moonlight.

Our orders were quite clear and I was not unduly perturbed when we set off in convoy. Lieutenant Parmenter was put in charge of the lorry in which Almond travelled. I led in my truck, with the lorry a few places behind. All went well until the Indians in front ran onto a minefield and turned in their tracks. The lorry was lost in the confusion and I never saw it again. I waited an hour and then continued as we formerly planned.

I feel sure that Almond is safe, though a prisoner of war. Thousands of Indians were captured in Mersa Matruh the next morning and I only hope that the lorry was among them. We lost our brigadier the same night, but his chances of being safe are very much less.

Almond, or George as he was known by everyone, was an extremely nice fellow. He always kept a steady head and produced beautiful work. I should be very grateful if you would tell me his new address as soon as they let you know.

George Almond, lower right, with companions from the King's Royal Regiment Pioneer Battalion HQ, Birmingham, 1940.

The captives had been handed over to the Italians. Lieutenant RH Parmenter, the Intelligence Officer, was flown to Italy almost immediately. The other prisoners were taken in stages to Benghazi by truck and loaded into the hold of a cargo vessel for the trip across the Mediterranean. On 26 July George Almond arrived at Taranto in southern Italy. After being held in camps PG 85 Tuturano, PG 87 Benevento, PG 66 Capua and PG 53 Sforzacosta, he was finally moved to the north-east.

In this fine account, George Almond recalls life as a prisoner:

In mid-May 1943 I was sent with 49 others to work detachment 17 of Camp 120 at Ponte San Nicolò, six kilometres from Padua, in the Veneto. We were housed in a small, new, brick structure, well equipped and comfortable. It was situated amid the fields of a large arable farm, where we worked quite happily. We were supervised by a farm worker. He amazed us by being permanently in bare feet, even on stubble. Although we never saw them, we could often hear children in fields not far away singing in marvellous harmony.

On the Armistice, five of us broke camp and went to ground in the nearby countryside. The others were Trooper R Gileney from Preston, drivers G Durndell of Salisbury and N Davey from Bradford, and Bombardier C Bryant of Grimsby. We came across a very steep-sided watercourse, which was probably the Brenta Canal according to a map of the district that I had access to some time later.

For the first month or so we remained hidden in the fields and ditches around the farm of Pietro Ferrara in Campagnola, until found by his children. With the help of family and friends, he provided us with food. Information was hard to come by owing to the language problem, but what we did obtain led us to believe that it would be only a matter of a few weeks before our forces arrived in the district.

However, we eventually discovered that the reports were unfounded and decided to remain hidden until conditions were more favourable for escape to our lines. We got in touch with some anti-Fascists in the nearby town of Piove di Sacco.

As a result, I was billeted above a wine shop at Via Garibaldi 35 with Emilio Raimondi, his wife, Maria, and their daughter, Veralba. She was five years older than I was. Her fiancé, Odo, was in Yugoslavia with the *Alpini*. I picked up quite a bit of conversational Italian while I was with the Raimondis and Veralba taught me one or two Italian songs.

Sometimes Emilio would take me with him in the evening when visiting friends. Once he took me to a cinema with one named Egidio. I sat between them somewhat nervously. After the newsreel, which showed the Axis version of current wartime events, the main feature was named *Louisa Sanfelice*, a lady who was obviously the target of Lord Nelson. He was portrayed as a swarthy villain with a black eye-patch.

I also remember on at least one occasion going for a cycle ride through the quiet countryside with one or two of the other British escapers and an Italian guide. We were near a village called Monteselice.

On Boxing Day 1943, the annual *Festa di Santo Stefano*, I was taken round the fairground, which was set up in the market square every year at that time. One of the roundabouts was playing the tune of *Roll Out the Barrel* to the words of an Italian song, *Rosamunda*.

I had a room containing a bed at the front of the building, above the shop and overlooking the main street. I spent most of the day there for security reasons. In keeping with this, my breakfast of bread and milk was brought to me whilst I was in bed. On one memorable occasion a German troop convoy which was passing through came to a halt. Veralba leant out of the window, chatting to the men. I was a little nervous, you can be sure!

Lunch would be perhaps a dish of *minestra* with *tagliatelle* pasta, and in the afternoon Maria and I would have a glass of Marsala and a hot potato. After one evening meal she proudly produced a two-ounce packet of Typhoo tea, but we usually drank non-vintage *vino*. When I left Piove, they gave me a bottle of *grappa*.

The flat had a small living room and kitchen where family meals were taken. The cooking area was in a curtained recess on one long side, which formed a good hiding place for me one day when a distant friend or relative came to visit from the other side of the peninsula. She was a Fascist sympathiser and I heard her referring to 'the poor Germans.' A squint through the curtain revealed that she had steel teeth.

When I went out and might meet the public I was told that I should if necessary explain my Italian accent by saying I was a

Siciliano, although my light hair was slightly more common in this part of the country.

In the evenings we used to listen to the overseas broadcasts from Britain in Italian. They often contained messages aimed at non-Fascists and Allied prisoners and evaders. One would hear either *'Ecco un commento di Candidus,'* [Here is a comment by Candidus] or *'Ora abbiamo il Colonnello Stevens'* [Now we have Colonel Stevens] and the messages would follow. One I remember was *'L' Adda passa per Lodi,'* [The Adda passes through Lodi]. Before leaving for our attempt to get into Switzerland, I was asked to have the message *'Giorgio pensa ad Ida'* [George thinks of Ida] transmitted as soon as possible if I succeeded in reaching England.

Gileney and Durndell went to a farm 12 kilometres out of town and Davey and Bryant to Correzzola, a village about 18 kilometres away. We continually tried to find suitable contacts with a view to arranging an escape expedition.

There were approximately 30 escaped prisoners of war hidden in the district, mostly South Africans. The chief organiser was a former Italian Army chaplain, Don Domenico Artero. He managed to get through the lines and spent about 30 days making arrangements for a motor torpedo boat to pick up prisoners from the coast at Mestre, below Venice. Unfortunately, these efforts failed and after January 1944 nothing more was heard of the padre. We then contacted the Communist underground movement.

On 13 February six of us left in an attempt to reach Switzerland, accompanied by guides. The others were Trooper Gileney, Driver Durndell, and three South Africans: Private L Macgregor and Lance Corporal K Bowker of the Transvaal Scottish Regiment, and Gunner J Turner.

We left on bicycles and spent three nights on a farm. The Raimondi family had equipped us with civilian clothing and I was also given 2,000 lire. We boarded the Venice-Milan express on the morning of 16 February. The train was compartmentalised, with sliding doors to a side corridor. No one seemed to take an interest in us and we stayed put until arriving at Milan. I had a short encounter with a young German soldier as I was emerging from the compartment. He was loaded with a full pack and rifle, so I naturally gave way.

Our guide must have been very efficient and experienced because we had no difficulty getting past the ticket barriers. We spent the night in Milan at the house of a priest, an agent of the underground organisation.

Next morning we travelled by electric train from Milan to Como. The train had open carriages with a central corridor. Sitting on an inside seat, I couldn't help glancing across from time to time at the British Army boot of Gileney, who was in a similar position on the other side in front of me.

Como station is a terminus and quite near to the lake. We went straight down to the shore. It was early in the day and I noticed how quiet it was. We got into a rowing boat that was waiting for us.

We were just pulling out when about 10 Fascists in civilian clothes and armed with pistols dashed down to the beach and captured us. We were each handcuffed to a guard and made to walk in the middle of the road. The one holding me was a big fellow with light ginger hair and a pronounced squint. What surprised me was that his hand was shaking noticeably. I heard later that, some days before, a body of partisans had come down from the hills and raided the train quite near there. We were taken to the party headquarters, searched and conveyed to the *Questura*, the police station.

I was shattered and scared at the sudden end of our expedition after getting so close to the Swiss border. I am sure we all were, but perhaps more so in my case, being rather a weakling of nine stone or so. This feeling gradually wore off. As the only one who had a reasonable smattering of conversational Italian, I had become a sort of leader of the band, under our guide of course, ever since leaving Piove di Sacco. Also, a more important concern took over: that we should be extremely careful not to say or do anything which might give a clue as to the identity of those who had cared for and equipped us back there.

We completed the usual Red Cross prisoner of war forms. An individual interrogation took place away from the cellblock. There were three or four men wearing civilian clothes in the room. None of them looked particularly Italian. Two hardly spoke at all and I somehow got the impression that one was a German.

The questioning was aimed solely at trying to find out who had helped in the escape attempt, using various devious gambits to obtain the information they were after, such as saying: 'You may as well talk, as all the others have.' The interrogators spoke in English and, although they were very determined, no violence was used or threatened. Their questions remained unanswered. At the end, I was sent back to the cell in a more relieved state than I had anticipated. We were taken to Como gaol and imprisoned for about a month.

While there, I met Lieutenant John Desmond Peck of the Australian Army. He had been recaptured while working with the Italian partisans. During interrogation his teeth had been broken and he was due to be tried in Milan. He requested that after the war I should enquire as to his fate, as he expected to be executed.

In our cell there were seven or eight people - the five of us, Lieutenant Peck, an Italian, and a Canadian soldier. He was a noisy, rumbustious character calling himself 'Red' Stewart, who proved to be rather a nuisance. On one occasion, we shut him up in the narrow space between the outer and inner doors of the cell.

We were subjected to the usual prison routine of daytime ablutions outside the cell and along the corridor and periods of exercise in the enclosed yard. Food was brought to the cell and sometimes items delivered through the small eye-level flap in the door. Towards the end of our stay, we were told that the trusty making the deliveries was a former Italian navy captain or commander who had sunk two Allied warships. How true this was, we had no means of knowing.

On 8 March the Germans moved us to Dulag 339 at Mantua. I am rather hazy about happenings on the day, merely that I was in the charge of a single armed German soldier - a quite pleasant but uncommunicative man. We travelled alone by train, in either an empty compartment or perhaps the guard's van.

The camp at Mantua was for me memorable only for the awfulness of the daily meal of soup. The consistency was such that with the thumb and forefinger you could make 'windows' with it. A gruesome pile of horses' skull bones with their large nostrils did not strain the imagination too much, for me at any rate.

Three weeks later, we were entrained for Stalag VIIA at Moosburg in Germany. We travelled via Trento, Bolzano and the Brenner Pass in the usual cattle trucks.

George Almond spent April and May at Stalag XIA Altengrabow, near Magdebourg, where he worked three days a week in forestry. In

June he was transferred to Arbeitskommando 340 at Gross Schierstedt, which is in the state of Saxony-Anhalt, and mined salt and coal until the spring of 1945.

By 14 April the Allied advance was drawing near. Small arms and shell fire had been heard overnight.

George Almond recalled:

> We left the camp for an organised march through the lines. There were 140 prisoners plus the guards. We arrived at Welbesleben, 12 kilometres away, at 22.20 hours after being sighted by RAF Typhoons on patrol.

Over two days the column travelled another 19 kilometres, but was then forced to retrace its steps 5 kilometres to Meisdorf. The original destination of Gernerode was now within the fighting zone.

> On 17 April the Yanks were only five kilometres away. Artillery fire was very near during the night.
>
> Next day, the Yanks entered and took Meisdorf at 13.30. Yippee! We got K-rations.
>
> I returned to England on 2 May and resumed my army service.

The soldier redeemed his promise to investigate the fate of John Desmond Peck, the escape agent and partisan. Enquiries continued into 1946. George Almond wrote to his superiors in March:

> The last I heard of Peck was when he left the prison at Como in Italy, in which we had both been held, for Milan, where he was to stand Grand Trial for sabotage before a German military court. This was on 4 March 1944.
>
> The reason I am making these enquiries is because, on being taken away, Peck asked me if ever I got back to England to make certain as to his fate, he expected to be shot, and then to notify his family, whose address is Crib Point, Victoria, Australia. So far I have not written to them, as I do not know whether he is alive or not.

The reply from the War Office related that Lieutenant Peck had got away and returned home safely. The Australian had been tried by the German military court in Milan and sentenced to death. But with the help of fellow prisoner Giuseppe Bacciagaluppi, head of the Resistance network for the assistance of Allied prisoners of war, he managed to talk his guards in the San Vittore gaol into sending him to a bomb disposal squad. The agent fled during an Allied air raid and escaped to Switzerland. John Peck was awarded the Distinguished Conduct Medal (DCM) for his gallantry in action.

It was also revealed after the war that Don Domenico Artero, George Almond and his friends' would-be saviour, who mysteriously disappeared in January 1944, had also been an Allied agent. On the Armistice in 1943, he rescued New Zealand prisoners from another work detachment of PG 120 Padua, number 8 at Fogolana. The priest led the party, which grew to 80, across the Po to the safety of a wood near Ravenna. Most were successful in crossing the lines. He was recruited by A Force, the Allied deception and escape secret organisation, and sent back to the Padua area. The planned naval pickup had come to grief owing to fog on the Venice lagoon. Shortly afterwards the Fascists put a 50,000 lire bounty on Don Artero's head. He fled, taking another party of prisoners with him. They crossed the border at Cassinone, Commune of Monteggio, in the Swiss canton of Ticino.

George Almond left the army in July 1946. He recalled:

> I soon started writing to the Raimondis and did exchange a few letters with Veralba. But due to the problems we experienced in coping with writing in each other's language, the correspondence did not last long, by mutual agreement.
>
> In the autumn of that year, I met the girl to whom I became engaged just before my release from the army, Mary Best. She is still my wife.
>
> I resumed my career as a semi-qualified architect's assistant, living near London, working in the city and studying to pass the final examinations to qualify as an architect. It was not until eight years later that I succeeded in this and, although I have had a reasonable career in my profession, I have never revisited Italy to revive old memories.

* * *

Quite the best tribute to the help given by the Italian people to Allied escaped prisoners of war and downed airmen is that by the British Prime Minister Winston Churchill, himself a successful escaper during the Boer War. In Volume V of his history, *The Second World War*, he wrote:

The insurgent movement in central and northern Italy here as elsewhere in occupied Europe convulsed all classes of the people. Not the least of their achievements was the succour and support given to our prisoners of war trapped by the armistice in camps in northern Italy. Out of about eighty thousand of these men, conspicuously clothed in battledress and in the main with little knowledge of the language or geography of the country, at least ten thousand, mostly helped by the local population with civilian clothes, were guided to safety, thanks to the risks taken by members of the Italian Resistance and the simple people of the countryside. [1]

The assistance from Italian civilians was usually spontaneous, localised and delivered by individuals or small groups. In contrast, official rescue work was planned, inter-service and inter-Allied.

British and American Military Intelligence worked through A Force, the deception and escape organisation attached to Allied Forces Headquarters. The organisation was known as IS9 (CMF) from 1944.

There was close cooperation with SOE, the British sabotage and subversion agency, the Secret Intelligence Service (SIS), the Special Air Service (SAS), and the various branches of the United States Office of Strategic Services, the OSS, especially Secret Intelligence, Special Operations, and Operational Groups, the equivalent of the British SAS.

The secret agencies relied on transport to infiltrate agents and ferry supplies to the Resistance. The main traffic was borne by private navies run out of Corsica and southern Italian ports until the summer of 1944. Afterwards, Mediterranean Allied Air Forces took the lead.

Sea missions on the eastern coast have usually received most attention. The Special Operations Executive, under its Italian cover name of No.1 Special Force, had its base at Monopoli, near Bari. The fleet operated out of Termoli and Manfredonia. Nearby Brindisi was the centre of OSS maritime - and aerial - operations. In 1945 both headquarters moved north to Tuscany, SOE to Siena in February and the OSS to Cecina in March.

The next chapter reveals the little-known story of clandestine operations in the west, from the Gulf of Genoa to the Tyrrhenian Sea.

NOTES

[1] Winston S Churchill, *The Second World War, Volume V*, pp 166-7.

5 Secret Sea Missions

Special Force's paranaval base on Corsica, codenamed Balaclava, ran operations into both Italy and France. It was led by the distinguished Arctic explorer Colonel Andrew Croft, DSO, OBE, and recipient of the Polar Medal, then a 37-year-old army captain.

In a speech to a conference of Special Force veterans and former members of the Italian Resistance, held at the University of Bologna in 1987, the colonel recalled the clandestine sea operations he led between December 1943 and July 1944:

> It is generally assumed that the vast majority of personnel trained by SOE for resistance duties in enemy-held countries were dropped by parachute. However, before Germany lost air supremacy, a larger proportion of these gallant men and women may well have been landed by Lysander aircraft and by sea. Such a comparative study has never been undertaken and no one will ever know the true facts, since so much information has been destroyed.
>
> At home, in England, I happen to have copies of reports of the 52 sea operations or sorties from bases in Corsica to the enemy-held coasts of south-east France and north-western Italy. I have them because I was never asked to destroy them. As a result, I am one of those lucky chaps who is able to give you information which is as accurate today as it was when written over 42 years ago.
>
> During the period December 1943 to July 1944, an SOE unit called Balaclava landed by sea into German-occupied territory as many as 75 people and brought out 21.
>
> The first clandestine sea operations carried out by SOE were those to the coast of Brittany in north-western France. These were run by Commander Gerard Holdsworth and Lieutenant Commander (now Sir) Brook Richards from their base in the Helford River in south-western England.
>
> After the invasion of North Africa in late 1942, these two well-known officers sailed their Brittany trawlers to Algiers - no mean feat of seamanship in itself. The pair created a great deal of difficulty for the Germans along the coasts of Tunisia. When that campaign had been completed, I joined their section after a spell with the Commandos.

The fact that I was an army officer in a naval section was perhaps unusual but typically British. As I had apparently acquired some experience in assault landings and also in handling small craft, canoes and rubber boats, I spent the next two months training personnel to use such craft effectively.

In August 1943, I had the good fortune to be sent off in the submarine HMS Seraph, skippered by Lieutenant Commander Jewell, to land radio sets on the Portofino peninsula. I have often wondered if these radio sets were ever found and used by the Italian Resistance. Precise compass bearings giving the location of the sets were sent to contacts in Italy.

Before the invasion of North Africa, that same British submarine had landed General Mark Clark and other Americans on the coast of Algeria for clandestine discussions with leading Frenchmen. Subsequently, Jewell's submarine also brought General Giraud out of the south of France.

My own three-week journey in Seraph was eventful. We torpedoed a German ship and were, in turn, attacked by Italian destroyers in sight of the town of Bastia in Corsica. This was not a pleasant experience as bits of steel from the exploding depth charges pinged against the hull of our vessel, now probably some 20 metres or so below the surface. However, by bouncing up and down in splendid Corsican mud we managed to survive the Italian onslaught.

On 9 September, the day after the Italian Armistice, we boarded an Italian merchant vessel. I acted as interpreter and managed to persuade the captain to alter course and proceed south towards the Allies. Later that day, we fired our one and only gun in anger - one of the very few submarines ever to do so. We managed to sink several German landing craft. Satisfied with that effort, I then won a bet with our captain for successfully navigating us home to Algiers.

On our return, I was instructed to sail to Corsica in the Brittany trawler FPV 2017 with an excellent crew from SOE and an American naval lieutenant as my second-in-command. Our role was to land trained organisers and radio operators with their sets and lightweight arms on enemy coasts. We were also, whenever practicable, to bring out any agents on the run from the Gestapo, as well as escaping prisoners of war. This trawler gave us mobility and was to prove invaluable as a temporary base, but above all for training purposes. To carry out effective operations we would have to depend upon fast craft from the navy.

We reached Corsica at the end of September 1943 to find that the Germans were about to evacuate the island through the port of Bastia. French troops, aided by Italian gunners, were helping to speed up this process.

Within the next month a great deal was accomplished. General de Gaulle visited the island and rapidly replaced the countless, incompetent Vichy officials. The French Army was made responsible for defence, the Americans for air operations and the Royal Navy for missions at sea.

While all this was going on, we acquired a small base at Calvi for sorties to France and a main headquarters in Bastia for Italian operations. Calvi was where Lord Nelson lost his right eye. It is also of interest to note that Napoleon Bonaparte, born in Ajaccio in 1769, became a French citizen as a result of an historical accident - the Genoese had held Corsica almost continuously since 1453 but had sold the island to France the year before Napoleon was born.

Our house in Bastia was large enough to accommodate our 12 operational men, a signal section, drivers, agents and conducting officers. Our operations room, run by Lieutenant Davies of 30 Commando, I made available to carefully selected members of SIS, OSS and the French *Bataillon de Choc*. Cooperation of this sort proved invaluable. Morale was also much improved as a result of German shelling, bombing and dropping of mines, together with invasion scares from Sardinia.

On 2 December our first operation took place when we landed blind, without any reception committee, two Italians and their radio sets north of La Spezia. With one of my men, I went ashore to carry out a reconnaissance before the agents were allowed to leave us. Later, and certainly on the larger operations, I considered it wiser to take two colleagues and two small boats, just in case. My aim was to avoid landing on beaches where the possibility of being blown-up in a minefield would not only be rather noisy but would also be a messy way of dying. Instead, I preferred rocky landings or the more unlikely places.

We confined our operations to the so-called non-moon period, which lasted for about 14 nights each month. The intervening time was fully occupied with boat repairs, improvements and experiments, whilst the operational personnel were taught new techniques and thoroughly trained in day and night manoeuvres.

Our staff of six Royal Corps of Signals personnel had daily radio schedules with Massingham, the SOE base in Algeria, and Maryland, SOE's No. 1 Special Force in Monopoli. They also, when permitted, kept in touch with agents in Italy.

The only fast operational craft available to the British Rear Admiral were Motor Torpedo boats (MTBs) and Motor Gun boats (MGBs) but these, although well armed, were rather slow and we much preferred the American PT [patrol torpedo] boats, 30 knot craft with experienced crews. Better still were the Italian MAS [*Motoscafi anti-sommergibili*] boats, capable of 40 knots but with crews whose performance at that time was not, understandably, entirely predictable. For instance, on a French commando operation the crew of MAS 541, with whom we had carried out several operations, liquidated their ginger-haired Captain Curolic, the British navigator, Lieutenant Dow, and all the Frenchmen. We in Corsica had assumed that the boat had hit a mine, but after the capture of Elba we learned that the crew had handed over the boat to the Germans in Porto Ferraio.

In mentioning this episode, I must emphasise that circumstances were not at that time straightforward for every Italian, especially naval personnel, many of whom could not face the possibility of being branded as traitors by their family and friends. There is an excellent example of this in Adrian Gallegos's book, *From Capri into Oblivion*.

These fast craft took us to within two kilometres or so of our destination, after reducing speed some 15 kilometres offshore to avoid being heard. On the few occasions when we landed arms, we used canvas-sided, flat-bottomed assault boats, otherwise rubber boats proved ideal. All boats were adapted for rowing and it was essential to muffle the oars with leather.

From training exercises, we knew that our boats with suitable camouflage paint could not be detected beyond 40 metres. On one operation I watched German troops, alerted by radar, noisily running down towards me while I carefully back-watered out to sea, fully confident in our camouflage but with a panic-stricken agent's revolver stuck in my chest. Rather unnecessary, I thought.

Viewed from the beach the first sign of an approaching boat is its shadow but this can be eliminated by using reflective aluminium paint. For camouflaging the upper parts of our boats, we found that, whether for night or day work, light greens or pinks were preferable. Such a combination seemed to be very effective when, on an operation to the Levanto area, two of my sergeants got left behind due to the sudden arrival of a German E-boat. To avoid compromising the three agents they had just landed, and the landing place itself, they decided to row out to sea and not wait the agreed five days for potential rescue. By sunrise, they were about eight kilometres from land and began in earnest to try to reach Corsica, some 160 kilometres to the south.

Their emergency rations consisted of two bottles of water, two flasks of rum, six bars of chocolate, two tins of corned beef and two Lyons 'twenty-four hour rations.' For three and a half days they saw no ship, only a few aircraft, and were visited by swordfish and whales. They also had to struggle at times against contrary winds and tides. Eventually, somewhat exhausted, they managed to reach the island of Capraia after rowing in a rubber boat some 150 kilometres in approximately 86 hours. I then received a nonchalant message: 'Beg leave to report safe arrival.'

The operations which gave me the most satisfaction were the two to Voltri pier in the western suburbs of Genoa, probably the best defended German-held port in the Mediterranean.

The first mission, Tail Lamp 2, took place on 6 February 1944 with two American PT boats, one of which broke down en route. On arriving in the target area shortly after midnight we were greeted with flares from nearby craft. Three vessels, less than two kilometres to starboard, were clearly seen through our binoculars. The American skipper was quite unperturbed and brought his boat to within two kilometres of the rendezvous at exactly 02.00, the time when the reception committee had promised to stand by.

No reception lights were visible, but I decided to take ashore three of the five agents who did not require to be met. I rowed ahead with Sergeant Coltman as a lookout, while Leading Seaman Miles followed 30 metres behind with the agents. We discovered that Voltri pier was not actually guarded, but about a hundred metres away on either side were what appeared to be machine gun emplacements with Germans giving away their position by smoking cigarettes.

Just as Miles was leaving the seaward end of the pier to row the agents ashore, an old woman came out of a house 20 metres from me carrying a lamp which she calmly placed on the ground, left for about eight seconds and then carried back into the house. I was so convinced that she had something to do with the reception committee that I shouted the codeword, 'Panzer.' A noise like the opening of a door came from the house, followed by a man's gruff voice speaking in Italian. I repeated the password, but the man, still remaining invisible, apparently went back in the house. We returned to the three agents, saw them safely under way and got back to the PT boat just five minutes before the captain had decided to leave the area. I still wonder what the old woman was doing with her lamp at 03.15 in the morning.

The second visit to Voltri pier, Operation Anstey, took place on 21 March 1944 with the objective of landing seven SOE agents and three SIS agents, an unusual combination. We made a good landfall at about 22.00 when I recognised directly ahead the dim outline of the foothills around Voltri. The chief SOE agent was convinced that the boat was heading for Arenzano and insisted that we altered course to starboard. As this manoeuvre would have taken us into the inner sanctuary of Genoa harbour and proved that the clearly visible Pole Star was not really due north at all, I took no notice and continued on our course.

I then manned a fast rubber boat, once more with Coltman as my armed lookout, and took care to have the critical agent safely in the stern. Miles followed, rowing a 5.5 metre flat-bottomed assault boat, with the nine remaining agents as passengers and plenty of room for their equipment, which included six radio sets. On arriving at Voltri pier, the chief SOE agent tried and failed to lower the ladder on the west side. Then to my surprise and delight, he went to fetch help from a friend in the guardhouse. A considerable swell was running with a rise and fall of at least a metre, so we used the rubber boat as a gangway. Apart from this, Operation Anstey was surprisingly easy and uneventful, as we saw no German guards or patrols, nor any ships. Ashore there were the usual lights from houses and only one searching behind Genoa itself.

By late July 1944, when I left Corsica for Algiers with seven of my best operational men to parachute into southern France, we had as a unit carried out 52 sorties since the previous December, with 24 proving successful. On all of these occasions, it is true to say that each radio operator came up on the air a few days later. Seventy-five agents and an unknown quantity of radio sets and light arms had been safely landed on Italian territory and we had brought back 21 men to Corsica. During all this time, we never had more than 12 trained operational personnel, yet on three nights we carried out three successful operations simultaneously.

In retrospect, it may be of interest to note the reasons for the 28 unsuccessful sorties since they give an insight into what actually happened: 7 failures due to bad weather; 7 failures due to hostile craft, usually E-boats; 6 failures due to faulty navigation; 4 failures due to no reception (3 of these were for A Force, the POW escape organisation); 2 failures due to engine breakdown; 1 failure due to a subsidiary operation which took too much time; and 1 failure due to enemy troops on the beach, caused by a radar alert.

Colonel Croft was awarded the DSO for his achievements in North Africa, Corsica and France during 1943-44. For understandable reasons, his 1991 memoir was entitled *A Talent for Adventure.* [1]

*   *   *

Secret sea missions south of Rome were led by Andrew Croft's SOE colleague Adrian Gallegos. He was born in Rome in 1907 of a Spanish father and an English mother and spoke five languages fluently. Gallegos took British nationality and worked in pre-war London as a Lloyd's underwriter before joining the Royal Navy.

His wartime adventures are recounted in the fine book entitled *From Capri into Oblivion* [2] and in this speech to the veterans' conference at the University of Bologna in 1987:

In August 1943 I was appointed by my commanding officer, Commander GA Holdsworth, as chief of the Advanced Naval Section of 'Massingham' in Sicily - a big command as the only other member of my unit was a wireless operator!

The commanding officer of the Advanced Military Section was Major Malcolm Munthe with whom I was to cooperate closely. At the time, I was lieutenant in the Royal Navy Volunteer Reserve (RNVR).

In Siracusa, I requisitioned, on the orders of Gerry Holdsworth, a schooner - the good ship 'Gilfredo.' It was intended to be used later on to ferry across the Adriatic armaments and supplies for the partisans in Albania and Yugoslavia. While we were in Sicily, Charles Macintosh and I took this vessel for a trial run in the Mediterranean. As it appeared to be seaworthy, I heard

53

afterwards that it was also used to ferry the two advanced parties of No. 1 Special Force to Brindisi.

On 6 September we set sail from Palermo in a Tank Landing Craft (LCT) for Salerno. On our second day out, we heard on the radio that the King of Italy and Marshal Badoglio, the Italian Commander-in-Chief and later Prime Minister, had reached an agreement with the Allies and so were out of the war. We hoped that this meant that we would have an unopposed landing. We were soon to be disappointed when, on the following day, we were greeted by Messerschmitts and Stukas.

We eventually landed at Salerno, so vividly described in Malcolm Munthe's *Sweet is War* [3]. A day later we made our way to Capri in Lieutenant Commander Quintin Riley's Infantry Landing Craft (LCI).

Capri was an ideal base for my type of operation as it was strategically placed opposite the Sorrento peninsula - at that time in no man's land. It was also close to Naples and the coastline to the north, still in enemy hands.

In addition to the British and American motor torpedo boats based there, the most suitable craft for my requirements, there was a flotilla of Italian MAS. They had reached Capri a week before my arrival after obeying the orders of their King to sail to the nearest Allied controlled port.

The flotilla had been based at Gaeta. On learning that the very few Germans on Capri had fled to Naples, they had pushed off to the island. The commanding officer was corvette captain Michelagnoli, who rose to the rank of admiral after the war.

During my stay in Capri, I was in close touch with three well-known Italians - Curzio Malaparte, the author and journalist, Alberto Tarchiani, who subsequently became the Italian Ambassador to Washington, and Alberto Cianca, who became a cabinet minister.

Although I did not know it at the time as we worked in very watertight compartments, Tarchiani and Cianca had been brought to Algiers by SOE. These illustrious men, dressed as privates in the British Army, were taken to Sicily by Charles Macintosh. Charles gives a very amusing account of this journey in his book, *From Cloak to Dagger*. From Sicily, they landed at Salerno with Malcolm before being moved to Capri, where they waited for the move to Rome.

With these stalwart men, Malcolm and I discussed the war and hatched up various plans. The first was to disarm the Fascist militia, 40 of whom had been left behind. We proposed to start a resistance movement on the mainland by arming a partisan group with the carbines and ammunition we had taken from the militia.

Before embarking on an operation of any importance, I had to refer to Admiral Morse as he was the senior naval officer in Capri. He referred me to Commodore Oliver, then Commodore Italy, with his flagship in Salerno Bay. This proved somewhat difficult, as he had never heard of SOE. However, I obtained his agreement, subject to certain precautions being taken.

I also had other schemes. One was to have the German general in command in Naples assassinated, and to blow up the oil storage tanks. With the help of our Italian friends we found a suitable Neapolitan to undertake these jobs. I took this gallant volunteer in an American gunboat to Amalfi in full daylight. Like Sorrento it was in no man's land, which meant that it was anybody's guess whether the Germans happened to be there or not. Although not based there, they frequently reconnoitred the area. On this occasion we were lucky and managed to land our man.

A day or so later, I was instructed to go over to Sorrento to rescue Benedetto Croce [4]. I was to go in an unarmed Italian naval launch as it looked like a pleasure craft. However, just in case, I wore uniform and carried a pistol and tommy gun. The newly elected mayor of Capri, Signor Brindisi, was in the boat with me and gallantly offered to accompany me to the Villa Tritone, where the Croce family lived. On stepping ashore, we enquired of several people if there were any Germans around but no one seemed to know for sure.

The most difficult part of this operation was to convince Benedetto Croce to return at once with me to Capri. Although his wife fully supported me, he thought that it was tantamount to running away. This discussion took some time, but he eventually agreed to leave with his two youngest daughters. Signora Croce asked to be collected the next day with her eldest daughter, as it would take some time to gather their belongings. So we left Sorrento under cover of darkness.

As I was booked for another job, Malcolm Munthe, with impeccable gallantry, went over the following day to collect the rest of the family. As Malcolm says in his book, it was lucky that the RAF had bombed a local bridge, so the guards at the Villa Tritone were otherwise occupied while this second extremely hazardous mission took place.

My last operation on Capri involved infiltrating into the Gulf of Gaeta an Italian who had fled from Naples and whom I recruited to carry out certain specific tasks as well as to reconnoitre the area. I managed to secure the services of an Italian MAS boat whose captain was 21-year-old *sottotenente* [second lieutenant] Luciano Marenco. We used the MAS as the crew knew the coastline intimately, having been based at Gaeta. This was important, especially for a night operation.

I rowed to the shore in a rubber dinghy, dropped the agent and rowed back to the MAS. When we were about eight miles from the coast we had just left, we went over an acoustic mine. Luckily we were travelling so fast that only the stern of the boat was damaged and two sailors slightly injured. Alas, as the boat was sinking, we had to abandon ship. There were 17 of us in three rubber dinghies in which we intended to make an unobserved night landing. But we found it impossible owing to the strong currents. We were met by the Germans when we eventually got to the shore.

The flotilla commander, Michelagnoli, had impressed on me before leaving Capri that, in the event of our being captured, we could tell our captors anything we liked but not that his MAS was carrying out an operation in conjunction with the Anglo-Americans. This was because the King of Italy and his breakaway government had not declared war against Germany and therefore we would be considered as irregular forces and liable to be shot on the spot under Hitler's *Fuhrerbefehl* [the 'Commando Order' of 1942 that 'all men operating against German troops in so-called commando raids ... are to be annihilated to the last man'].

So Marenco and I concocted a story that we were defecting from the Anglo-Americans to join the Fascists and Germans. I then sent my uniform to the bottom of the sea and pretended that I was an Italian sailor. I could get away with this as I am bilingual in Italian, and the whole crew were informed of the plot. We also reckoned that, after a while, we could have disappeared in Italy and rejoined our units.

But it was not to be as, on reaching Regina Coeli in Rome, Marenco, faced with press reporters and photographers, felt that he could not stand being publicly labelled as the captain of a unit which had defected from the Italian Navy. Thus, instead of our cover story, he stated that we had been patrolling on behalf of the Anglo-Americans. All of us were then promptly sentenced to death.

However, Marenco's father and others brought pressure to bear on the Germans and we were declared prisoners of war. They kept us in Regina Coeli for 56 days, when the crew and I were sent off to Germany. Alas, we lost contact with Marenco as he was sent to a prison camp for officers.

We were taken to the prisoner of war camp at Moosburg. The camp was administered by French personnel, so I was able to talk quite openly. After telling them that I wanted to escape they made it possible for me to get to Munich where, they said, I would be able to contact people who would help me on my way. Before leaving, I asked the crew of the MAS what they would like to do and they all said 'farming' to be away from towns. This I was also able to arrange.

Eventually, in April 1944, I escaped from Munich. After many vicissitudes, including being recaptured in the summer, I reached a partisan group near Pontremoli in the Apennines above La Spezia. The Commander was Colonel Fontana who had with him a BLO called Major Gordon Lett, the author of *Rossano*.

I stayed with this group for about six weeks. Lett sent a signal to No. 1 Special Force HQ who confirmed my bona fides and instructed me to report to Rome as soon as possible. I asked to stay with the partisans as the food was better there than at Monopoli, but this was refused. Eventually an opportunity arose for me to join a very small escorted group of ex-POWs and we successfully crossed the lines in November 1944.

After a short spell in England, I was appointed second-in-command to Major Charles Macintosh at TAC HQ [Tactical Headquarters] in Fiesole. We shared the villa with the SAS and were in direct contact with the British liaison officers in the field. While I was there, I was promoted to lieutenant commander.

I did a parachute course as I and some others were earmarked to be dropped to partisan formations in the north as soon as the much-heralded spring offensive started. When this happened, the military advanced so fast that we went in with the army by jeep instead of being parachuted.

The Armistice was signed in May 1945 and that was the end of the war, for me.

After the liberation of Corsica in October 1943, the American Office of Strategic Services (OSS), the forerunner of the Central Intelligence Agency (CIA), also established a base at Bastia to infiltrate agents and supplies into south-eastern France and north-western Italy.

The United States equivalent of the British SAS, the Operational Groups (OGs), had their base at Ile Rousse. The Italian unit was eventually designated Company A of the 2677th Regiment OSS (Provisional).

The company used American PT or British MT boats sailing out of Bastia to conduct reconnaissance and sabotage of targets on the mainland. The islands of Capraia and Gorgona were also captured and outposts established to observe enemy shipping and to provide weather reports and early warning for Air Force units stationed in Corsica.

A specially adapted PT boat was used to mount search and rescue operations for airmen reported downed in the sea. Spitfires flown by American personnel provided air cover till the mission was completed.

On 1 September 1944 the Operational Groups moved to Siena on the mainland and were redesignated Company A of the 2671st Special Reconnaissance Battalion, Separate (Provisional). The new designation eliminated the reference to the OSS to underline that the Operational Groups were military and operated in uniform behind enemy lines. If captured, their men were entitled to the protection of the 1929 Geneva Convention as prisoners of war. The enemy did not always respect this code.

The summer proved to be the high point for special operations based on sea missions. Thereafter they lost out in number and importance to those reliant on air power, the subject of the next two chapters.

NOTES

[1] Andrew Croft, *A Talent for Adventure*, Worcester: The SPA Ltd, 1991.

[2] Adrian Gallegos, *From Capri into Oblivion*, London: Hodder and Stoughton, 1959.

[3] Malcolm Munthe, *Sweet is War*, London: Gerald Duckworth, 1954.

[4] At the time of the rescue, Benedetto Croce was 77 years old. He was the foremost Italian philosopher, literary critic and historian of the twentieth century. The patriot was wartime president of the Italian Liberal Party. The party, whose other leader was Count Alessandro Casati, was right wing and royalist, but critical of King Victor Emmanuel III.

6 Special Operations

United States veterans of the Italian OSS section and the partisan associations jointly promoted a conference in Venice in 1994 on the theme of 'The Americans and the War of Liberation in Italy - Office of Strategic Services (OSS) and the Resistance.'

Retired United States Air Force lieutenant colonel Jon Walter Bradbury made this keynote speech on 'The Complexities of Special Operations.':

There was in World War II a great lack of efficient organisation and procedure in both Resistance and special air operations, albeit for somewhat different reasons. And yet, despite what at the time seemed utter confusion, very great contributions were made towards the successful outcome of the war and the liberation of Italy and the rest of Europe. These were accomplished through the persistent efforts of those who overcame bureaucratic obstacles, petty jealousies and differing agendas. Unfortunately, much of the effort is not reflected in official records, and organisational histories are frequently incomplete and sometimes inaccurate. Thus, the full history will remain unrecorded.

The concept of special air operations was not a completely new one in World War II - although judging by the way we went about it, one would think that it was.

Apparently, the first effort was as early as the Franco-Prussian War (1870-1) when documents and agents were flown in a balloon out of Paris above the surrounding Prussians. And, according to a newspaper report of 9 July 1915, an Italian pilot landed and later picked up agents behind the lines in World War I. The Germans claimed the Allies landed soldiers in civilian clothes in German territory for sabotage. The Italian victory over the Austrians in 1918 at Vittorio Veneto was credited to the report of an Italian agent flown from an Italian airfield and dropped behind the lines. Agents were landed, picked up and dropped by air throughout World War I.

As it was in World War I, the characteristic of clandestine air operations in World War II was infiltration, extraction and sustaining of personnel in enemy territory. Prime Minister Winston Churchill stated the mission simply in 1940 for both the

European Resistance and Allied special operations: 'Set Europe ablaze.' I submit, however, that Churchill did not mean the actual burning of the Continent. What he meant was to light the fires of patriotism and kindle the flames of resistance in occupied Europe.

There were four basic missions:

(1) Gather and transmit intelligence.
(2) Rescue Allied airmen.
(3) Conduct psychological efforts to expand anti-Nazi opposition within the populace.
(4) Engage in sabotage and harassment of the enemy.

To support the Resistance organisations, the air forces' units developed a series of tactics to accomplish the objectives.

The compromise of Resistance members or agents was a basic concern, thus the preservation of secrecy became of utmost importance in both planning and execution of missions - far more so than for conventional air units. Because of the covert nature of the missions every effort was made to avoid enemy detection by flying primarily by night at low altitude. Night navigation in World War II was a major problem for aircrews trying to find drop or landing zones identified only by flash lights or perhaps small fires. Reliable electronic aids were almost non-existent, thus map reading and dead reckoning had to be used. This meant that the 17 days each month when the moon provided sufficient light to see the terrain were the nights of major efforts.

The B-24 Liberators used in special operations received more modifications, with installation of an opening ('Joe hole') in the floor where the ball turret had been removed, affixing flame suppressers on engine exhausts and removing all unnecessary items such as oxygen equipment. To avoid attracting attention, gunners manning the only two gun turrets remaining were ordered not to fire their weapons unless fired upon.

From the beginning, special operations were not looked upon with favour in either the Royal Air Force or the United States Army Air Force (USAAF), or for that matter by the ground forces. The British Special Operations Executive (SOE) was created in July 1940 and the Office of Strategic Services (OSS) was established in 1942. Both Air Chief Marshal Sir Arthur 'Bomber' Harris and General Henry 'Hap' Arnold felt the war could be won by strategic bombardment and wanted every bomber they could get for that purpose.

Thus the evolution of both RAF and USAAF special operations was both difficult and lengthy. By mid-1941 only a very few aircraft were assigned to RAF special operations and it was not until September 1943 that an American special flight section of three B-17 Flying Fortresses was detailed to OSS Algiers and flew its first mission on 20 October. Four days later, a special operations group, codenamed the Carpetbaggers, was established in Britain and began training with an RAF special duties squadron. It had taken 21 months of continuous effort to get this token assignment - and the organisational and operational confusion was still ahead regarding the problems of who does what and how they do it.

In a sense, the American efforts to develop a special mission capability in Italy and the Balkans mirrored the endeavours of the anti-Fascist elements to effectively resist Mussolini and Hitler. Unlike other occupied countries, the Italian Resistance had its origins long before the beginning of the war.

Although Mussolini did not come to power until after the March on Rome on 9 October 1922 and did not outlaw all non-Fascist political organisations until 1926, an anti-Fascist weekly had appeared in 1922 and an underground had begun developing in 1925.

The Resistance was largely unorganised and even though SOE agents were sent in after June 1940 to make contacts, the British knowledge of the situation in Italy was inadequate and the teams ineffective. Consequently, the British, until after the Armistice of September 1943, felt that the Resistance was not organised or large enough to warrant the dropping of supplies.

For the Americans the priority was always France in anticipation of invasion. By 1943 the OSS had completed plans for their operations, but lacked air transport, which the Mediterranean Air Command and 8th Air Force in Britain refused to provide. The OSS plans had been approved by the Joint Chiefs of Staff in Washington and the Commander-in-Chief of Allied Forces, General Eisenhower, but General Carl A Spaatz in the Mediterranean and General Ezra Eaker in Britain maintained they could not spare aircraft for special operations. In Washington, General William 'Wild Bill' Donovan continued to press General Arnold and the Joint Chiefs of Staff to direct the Army Air Force to supply the needed aircraft - 12 bombers for Britain and 6 for Algiers. With continued rebuffs, in the summer of 1943 Donovan sought and received the support of General Spaatz's close friend and chief of staff, General Edward P Curtis. Meanwhile in Britain, General Eaker was given a tour of OSS/SOE facilities and Tempsford, home of the RAF special duties squadrons. Eaker, though now supporting the concept of air special operations, felt he could not spare the aircraft.

It was at this juncture that US Navy Aviation assumed the anti-submarine activities being performed by USAAF B-24s out of Britain. This, in October 1943, made available these aircraft, which were not equipped for high altitude bombing. Thus, the Carpetbaggers came into existence.

The sudden availability of uncommitted aircraft in Britain, and the influence of a mutual friend, resulted in General Donovan getting the beginnings of the special air operations he wanted. But there was still a long way to go.

In the Italian Resistance, which grew out of the outlawed political parties, there were also difficult problems of organisation for common purposes. Just as proponents of Allied special air operations required time to overcome the difficulties of achieving a common purpose and coordinated effort, so too did the Italian Resistance leaders such as Giulio Nicoletta, Guido Quazza, Ferruccio Parri and others. They sought a unified, effective Resistance force, as General Donovan sought organised, effective special air operation units. All were frustrated by intransigence and, as they saw it, lack of vision.

After the fall of Mussolini the political parties began to come together, with the Committee of National Liberation *[Comitato di Liberazione Nazionale* or *CLN]* in Naples providing the example in September 1943. It was composed of six parties. Gradually committees appeared throughout central and northern Italy.

These developments coincided with the decision to give greater support to the Resistance and to move the RAF Halifaxes and B-24s for special air operations from Blida, North Africa, to Brindisi, which was accomplished by January 1944.

At Blida, the USAAF three B-17s had been augmented by three B-25 Mitchells (which were useless except for secondary operations) and designated the 122nd Liaison Squadron. It moved to Manduria in south-eastern Italy in late December 1943.

In January 1944 General Eaker was transferred from Britain to take command of the Mediterranean air forces. By now he was a strong supporter of special operations and was appalled to find the sad state of affairs in North Africa and Italy. He immediately began initiating messages to General Arnold asking for authority to organise a legitimate special air operation, since he would not allow the existing slipshod arrangements to continue. This resulted in a long, bitter dispute between the two. As with the Italian Resistance movement, it became a matter of politics, negotiations and influence to resolve competing interests and agendas. Shortly, many other senior officers were drawn into the controversy in support of Eaker's interest to provide a greater Army Air Force special operations capability. RAF Air Marshal Sir John Slessor, Eaker's deputy, dispatched a cable to Air Chief Marshal Charles Portal, British Chief of Air Staff, to pressure Arnold - which he did. Apparently, Arnold never understood the nature of the special operations request and disapproved of it.

General Eaker refused to give up and generals Eisenhower and Donovan advised the Deputy Supreme Commander, Mediterranean, General Devers, that they strongly supported Eaker. Generals Devers and Eaker immediately dispatched a message to General George C Marshall, Army Chief of Staff and Arnold's boss. Eaker also wrote to General Benjamin M Giles, Chief of Air Staff. Only generals Arnold and Spaatz were opposed, while arrayed against them were - Churchill, Eisenhower, Wilson, Donovan, Portal, Slessor, Devers and Eaker. General Marshall now referred the issue to the Combined Chiefs of Staff, who decided in favour of Eaker. So finally, on 9 March 1944, Eaker was authorised to create a special operations squadron. The 885th Bombardment Squadron (Special) was activated with the three B-17s and an additional 12 B-24s at Blida.

In Britain, the Carpetbaggers, despite many changes of unit designation and air bases, had become an efficient, experienced special operations unit with eventually 64 aircraft in four squadrons. On 23 April 1944 the Carpetbagger commander, Lieutenant Colonel Clifford Heflin, flew a B-24 to Algiers to advise the 885th Squadron on aircraft modification and training for special operations.

After the liberation of southern France, where the 885th Squadron had been making drops, the unit was moved to Brindisi in September 1944 and the priority changed to supplying the Italian Resistance, while the RAF would concentrate on the Balkans.

By now the number of committees of national liberation had increased in northern Italy and had evolved into a more or less cohesive network. The Milan CLN provided leadership for the Committee of National Liberation of Upper Italy (CLNAI). USAAF special operations still had some confusion to resolve.

In November 1944 the 62nd Troop Carrier Group (TCG) was assigned to special operations, with its C-47s flying out of Siena. In January 1945 the 64th TCG replaced the 62nd, flying out of Rosignano and Tarquinia. Although involved in supplying the Italian Resistance and actually landing in occupied northern Italy a few times, the C-47 efforts were directed mainly towards the Balkans. In December 1944 the 859th Carpetbagger Squadron arrived on detached service from Britain to help the 885th Squadron at Brindisi and later at Rosignano.

By the time the last special operations mission was flown to northern Italy on 7 May 1945, the immense complexities of resolving the conflicts of special operations organisation and Resistance cooperation and coordination had finally been settled. Both now had become viable and efficient members of the same team, which contributed immeasurably to the termination of the war. A major general, WA Stawell, commanded Special Operations Mediterranean Theatre of Operations, and Ferruccio Parri, a noted Resistance leader, headed a provisional Italian government.

The combined Carpetbagger losses for both the Mediterranean and European theatres were 28 aircraft and 223 crewmen. Of these, 15 crewmen were lost flying out of Brindisi. In terms of bomber aircraft, the total diversionary cost to the USAAF of the World War II special operations effort, which caused so much controversy, was 47 front-line bombers.

In June 1945 Brigadier General Charles T Myers, commanding officer of the United States Twelfth Air Force, wrote a letter of commendation to his counterpart in the 2677th Regiment OSS. In reference to the Italian operational groups, the message reads:

Company A willingly assumed the extra burden of exfiltrating by land and sea airmen of both 12th Air Force and Desert Air

Force, even though it taxed them in the accomplishment of their primary mission. Their complete cooperation in assisting airmen to evade capture by the enemy included direct instructions to their agents to render all possible aid: to help with money, food, clothing, hiding places and guides.

The Operational Groups of the OSS spearheaded guerrilla warfare behind enemy lines. The units were composed of second-generation Italian-American soldiers. They were given commando training and parachuted into occupied territory to harass the enemy and encourage and support local resistance organisations. There were 29 missions.

Captain Albert Materazzi was the Operations Officer. He recalled:

The Italian Operational Group was the first to be activated and was designated Group A. Recruitment from other Army units began in April 1943. After training, the group was transferred to Station X, the OSS base near Algiers, at the end of August. It was planned that parachute training would be given, but it had barely started when operations began.

One group went to Italian-occupied Corsica, together with a French force, to liberate the island in conjunction with the local *Maquis*. They also harassed the German 90th Panzer Division, which was evacuating Sardinia by moving up the east coast of Corsica to the port of Bastia.

Another group was parachuted into south-eastern Italy to help recover Allied prisoners released by the Italians upon their surrender on 8 September. The officer commanding the group was captured and some of the men remained behind the lines for almost nine months.

OG personnel also jumped blind into Sardinia to notify the Italian command of the Armistice and pass on orders from their new government to cooperate with the Allies.

In mid-October the rest of Group A moved from Station X to Ile Rousse in Corsica. This became the base for nine months.

Meanwhile the Allied Armies in Italy moved slowly up the peninsula. Rome was not liberated until 4 June 1944. Two days later the Allies landed in Normandy. Seven of the most experienced divisions fighting in Italy were transferred to the Seventh Army for landings in southern France. Thus the weakened armies remaining were unable to breach the heavily fortified German Gothic Line to take Bologna and break into the

Po Valley. The winter of 1944-45 was one of the worst in Italian history. The GIs asked: 'Whatever happened to sunny Italy?'

During the Allied advance to the Gothic Line some excellent partisan bands were overrun and proved to be very valuable in tactical situations. The bands in the north occupying the mountains were in a position to attack the German lines of communication. Obviously they had to be supplied and their operations coordinated with those of the regular army forces. This was the job for which the OGs were created.

At the end of August, Group A was transferred to Siena. Now designated Company A, 2671st Special Reconnaissance Battalion, it was placed under the operational control of G-3 Special Operations, 15th Army Group.

In mid-August the first military mission in uniform was dropped in the Liguria area, near the important port of Genoa. It consisted of an OG section of 2 officers and 13 enlisted men.

By 2 May 1945, when the Germans formally surrendered, in spite of bad weather and the limited availability of aircraft and supplies, there were 10 OG missions with a total of 120 men in strategic areas of northern Italy.

In some cases as much as two weeks elapsed after the surrender before being overrun by Allied troops and the arrival of Allied military governors. In the interim, food and essentials for the civilian population were dropped to the OG teams. They and the partisans administered the areas and maintained order. Recalcitrant Fascists and Germans suspected of being war criminals were rounded up and arrested.

During the winter, when parachute operations were difficult, the OGs were used for a variety of tasks. The responsibility for partisan bands at the front in tactical situations belonged to the OSS and to the Fifth and Eighth Army Detachments. On the western front, the Fifth Army detachment did not have sufficient personnel, so 5 OG officers and 20 OG enlisted men were loaned until the unit came up to full strength.

Early in 1945 a packing station was opened at an airbase near Leghorn and a Troop Carrier Group flying Dakotas (C-47s) was stationed there to resupply forward positions. Lacking dispatchers, OGs performed that dangerous mission until Airforce personnel could be trained.

In northern Italy OG missions regularly furnished weather reports and bomb assessments to the Air Force and provided assistance to downed airmen.

The numerous operations of support to the regular military operations in Italy, plus the special OG operations with the partisans, drew unanimous praise from the Allied commanders.

In recognition, 2 Distinguished Service Crosses, 20 Silver Star Medals, 10 Legion of Merit Medals, 30 Bronze Star Medals, 25 Air Medals, 8 with Oak Leaf Clusters, and 29 Purple Hearts were awarded to individual members of the unit.

The company was honoured with the Presidential Distinguished Unit Award on 18 July 1946. The commendation reads:

Company A is cited for outstanding performance of duty in action against the enemy in Italy from 15 April to May 1945.

The company, composed of officers and enlisted men who volunteered for extra hazardous duty in the conducting of operations behind enemy lines, engaged in extensive operations in Italy under the direction of the 15th Army Group Headquarters.

These men, organised into small operational groups, were infiltrated behind the enemy lines by parachute and, maintaining contact with headquarters by radio, organised extensive partisan forces.

In the final phase of the offensive of the 15th Army Group, they led these partisan forces in all-out attacks. The officers and enlisted men of Company A, despite the constant danger of attack and capture, by their courageous leadership and participation in the operations of these Resistance forces were instrumental in causing them to organise and attack the enemy and were a constant inspiration to them, thus reflecting great credit on themselves and on the Armed Forces of the United States.

In a speech entitled 'Italian-American Operational Groups of the OSS,' another of the American veterans at the Venice conference, former OSS liaison officer Emilio Caruso, recalled that many missions were sent into northern Italy as the war escalated in the winter of 1944. The official log of Company A was full of these types of activities:

New missions; supply drops; unsuccessful attempts because of weather conditions; reports of injuries; the loss of men killed in action; supply drops including medical supplies to partisan organisations; leave for men who had spent more than four months behind the lines; the aid given to downed airmen; radio contacts lost and re-established; men sent to the Mountain Warfare Training Centre; training in skiing and mountain climbing; more injuries in training and in action; money dropped to our missions in sealed containers; money delivered to partisan commanders; a Bronze Star awarded; a Silver Star awarded; heart-warming reports of praise for officers and enlisted men behind the lines; Purple Hearts for the wounded; a field commission to 2nd Lieutenant for an enlisted man; reinforcements sent to various missions; the crashing and burning of a plane, killing all on board; a B-24 flying in supplies shot down; report that captured men were released from a prison camp - and more of the above.

* * *

Throughout German-occupied Europe air supply held the key to resistance. Professor Michael Foot, the official historian of SOE, wrote that 'arms are to active resisters what rain is to farmers - nothing can be done without them.' And most arms had to be delivered by parachute. 'This involved much danger on the ground for the reception committees. It also involved several thousand airmen, flying and servicing the special duty squadrons.'

The extent of the Allied airlift to the Italian partisans was revealed to a select few in Britain by a 1948 publication, *The Secret History of SOE: The Special Operations Executive 1940-1945,* written by Professor William Mackenzie. The book, commissioned by the Cabinet Office, was in effect the in-house history of the wartime secret service and remained classified for over 50 years. The statistics show that Italy was the third most important destination for supplies in Europe, only being exceeded by France and Yugoslavia.

Christopher Woods, SOE agent and chronicler, related that Special Force claimed to have provided 2,145 tons of supplies to the Italian Resistance by air from 1 January 1944. The breakdown of items included nearly 25,000 Stens, over 2,500 Brens and other light machine guns, nearly 10,000 rifles, 225 tons of explosives, 450 kilometres of fuse, 300,000 each of detonators and primers, 11,320 suits of battledress, and 27,665 pairs of boots.

The figures for the airlift head the next chapter.

7 Secret Air Missions

Official British statistics state that Allied aircraft delivered a total of 4,469 tons of supplies to the Italian partisans during World War Two.

The figures for the individual quarters are as follows:

1943

3rd Quarter	4
4th Quarter	<u>1</u>
Total...	<u>5</u>

1944

1st Quarter	92
2ndQuarter	398
3rd Quarter	650
4th Quarter	<u>780</u>
Total...	<u>1,920</u>

1945

1st Quarter	1,669
2nd Quarter	<u>875</u>
Total...	<u>2,544</u>
Grand total...	<u>4,469</u>

Similar calculations published in the United States in 1945 in the Allied Forces Headquarters' official report, *History of Special Operations (Air) in the Mediterranean Theatre*, have a slightly higher figure for the total of supplies dropped at 5,907 tons.

This source also reveals that 538 agents were delivered to the field and that there were 4,280 individual aircraft sorties undertaken during the airlift. Of these 2,652, or 61.96 per cent, were successful.

The results reflect the skill and bravery of the airmen and the partisans on the ground. Both operated in the most hostile conditions.

The rebels even constructed a large airfield deep in the mountains of northern Italy. Italian Army junior officers provided leadership.

On Sunday, 19 September 1943, German troops attacked a thousand men of the Italian Fourth Army who had taken shelter in the mountains above Boves in the province of Cuneo in Piedmont.

After encountering fierce resistance, the SS launched savage reprisals against civilians. The troops burnt 350 houses and killed 24 inhabitants. At the turn of the year, another 59 residents and partisans were slain and the village again torched. In 1961 Boves was awarded the Italian Gold Medal for Civilian Valour, and two years later with the military medal.

The Resistance bands created by regular army officers provided the nucleus for one of the largest partisan formations in Piedmont, the *Autonomi,* or Independents. Most of the soldiers were monarchists. They declared that they were fighting in the name of the king, His Majesty Victor Emmanuel III. The brigades were open to everyone who shared these ideals. On 13 October 1943 the royalist government in the south declared war on Germany, and Italy was granted the status of co-belligerent by the Allies, making the soldiers' duty even clearer.

The leader of what developed into the Alpine Divisions was Enrico Martini, 'Mauri,' a 32-year-old career soldier from Mondoví. He had served with the *Alpini* in Africa and on the 1943 Armistice was a staff officer with the Army High Command in Rome. The major took part in the defence of the capital and after it was occupied by the Germans returned to Piedmont to organise armed resistance in the mountains.

The independent brigades operated in the Cuneo, Langhe and Monferrato areas. The officers created an intelligence service which liased with that of the Italian Armed Forces in the south, the *Servizio Informazioni Militari (SIM)*, and with the Allied secret services. The partisan formation was viewed very positively in those circles and as a result received regular airdrops of weapons, ammunition and supplies.

On 16 June 1944 a local commander reported the arrival of a supply drop to the regional liberation committee:

During the night of 6-7 June at 00.15 an aircraft dropped supplies in the Bra area. Owing to the need to hide all the material as quickly as possible it has not been possible to list everything that has been sent, but nothing has been lost.

Twenty-six parachutes were recovered with their loads. The contents were: 6 containers with 554 Sten guns; 1 container of supplies; 1 container with 10 pistols, maps, etc; 10 containers of explosives; 1 container with clothes; 4 containers of ammunition and 3 containers with hand grenades.

The next morning, 3 containers were found without parachutes near a farmhouse and outside the area of the drop.

In conformity with the orders of 'Major Mauri,' some of the supplies have been sent to the Marco band.

In July, the Special Force Flap Mission parachuted into the Ellero Valley, south of Mondoví and Cuneo. The team was led by 'Major Temple,' Neville Lawrence Temple Darewski. Second-in-command was Arne Flygt, a Swede. The Wireless Operator was Bert Farrimond.

Flygt was quickly captured by the Germans. His brother-in-law, Captain Michael Lees, was sent in as replacement. He was accompanied by a journalist from *The Toronto Star*, Paul Morton, and by Geoffrey Long, a war artist from South Africa. The team was dropped too near to Turin. Fortunately, they were taken under the wing of the Communist partisans of the Sixth Garibaldi Division. They provided guides to Major Mauri's headquarters. From there the quartet trekked to Major Temple's base, a mountain hut above Prea.

Captain Lees supervised supply drops and training for the partisans. He recalled: 'In a short time they showed signs of becoming a trained and efficient striking force. I looked forward hopefully to the day when, with the Allied armies pushing forward, we would be able to sweep down and clean up the plains.'

After several weeks at Major Temple's HQ, Michael Lees received orders to evacuate two important members of the CLN, Professor Giovanni Bessone (Salvi) and another known as Piva, so that they could report to the Allies on events in the north. He recalled:

I set off from Prea with a party of 16 including escaped POWs, one or two American pilots and the gentlemen of the press, Morton and Long. After two days we reached Pigna, having crossed the Maritime Alps. I continued immediately on the last stage of the route to Menton through the German lines. Because of the mountainous nature of the country and the lack of any guides or reconnaissance of the route, I limited the party to five, including of course the two CLN members; an Italian wireless operator, Sergeant Balestri; and Fred Dobson, an escaped POW, who acted as interpreter.

The group of 16 was insufficiently fit, trained or disciplined to undertake what promised and proved to be a very tough crossing.

However, I left the best man of all, an ex-guardsman POW, William McClelland, to help Morton and Long, and, more by luck than good judgement, I set in motion plans for the rest to be evacuated by boat which miraculously worked. Morton, Long and McClelland at least came by that route shortly afterwards.

We stumbled on and shot up a German observation post on the way through. I was able to deliver the CLN members to HQ Bari precisely on schedule as ordered. [1]

A future general of the *Alpini,* Renato Pensa, was a partisan with Major Mauri's divisions. The general made a speech entitled 'Landing Fields for Allied Aircraft in Partisan Areas' to the conference of American veterans and ex-partisans held in Venice in 1994. He recalled:

I fought as a partisan in the Cuneo area in Piedmont, on the Maritime Alps in Val Casotto, at Boves and on the Langhe, with the 1st Group of Alpine Divisions of the independent formations of Mauri (*Alpini* Major Enrico Martini).

'Independent' because we were not tied to any political party. We were coming out of a dictatorship and felt free. We did not have any political awareness as yet and therefore wanted to reflect before taking any decisions. We had, however, made one important choice. We were against the Fascists and the Germans, and we intended bringing back freedom and democracy. The priority for us at that moment was the armed conflict.

The British were the first to join forces with the Resistance and to send missions to the independent formations of 'Mauri.'

Later on, OSS American missions appeared. In the intelligence field we had contact with the organisation of Aminta Migliari. In the operational sector, OSS Mission No. 2677 'Morristown,' guided by Maurizio Fracassi, parachuted in to Soglio Monferrato on 16 January 1945 to one of our brigades which operated in the Monferrato area.

Elsewhere in Piedmont and Lombardy there was the mission of Major Holohan and Lieutenant Icardi in Val d' Ossola, one with the Franchi organisation of Edgardo Sogno, later recipient of the Gold Medal for Military Valour and an ambassador, and another in Val Chisone with the independents of 'Marcellin.' They received supplies across the French border with crossings at 3,000 metres, which required considerable mountain climbing experience.

However, I want to particularly highlight the activities of brave and skilled American pilots who operated beyond their lines with large planes. They landed on a short, grassy strip constructed in a narrow valley. There was little chance of a second pass should the landing prove impossible due to a tail wind or obstacles on the ground.

In that period our fighting force consisted of about 6,000 men equipped with light arms, who not only carried out guerrilla warfare but also occupied and defended vast areas and whole villages. 'Commander Mauri' and Major Temple (Neville Darewski), head of the British mission, had agreed that a landing strip in partisan country would greatly simplify the problems which beset the Piedmont Resistance. The field would ensure easy and rapid connections with southern Italy and the Allied HQ, the early repatriation of countless Allied soldiers who were being sheltered by partisan formations and the transfer of the most seriously wounded to the safer and better equipped hospitals of liberated Italy.

After carrying out a survey, 'Major Temple' and Commander Poli (Piero Balbo), leader of the 2nd Langhe Division, chose a series of fields along the right bank of the Bormida, between Vesime and Cortemilia, in the province of Cuneo and Asti. The zone was enclosed by hills and obstructed by a farm building. It was demolished and rebuilt nearby.

Hundreds of men equipped with shovels and pickaxes levelled the ground and then a good number of oxen and horses dragged stone rollers to compact it. Lieutenant Gio (Giorgio Caffa) of the Engineer Corps and the surveyor Pasquale Balaclava were responsible for the work under the guidance of Pilot Officer Piero Ghiacci of the 2nd Langhe Division.

Within about 10 days a 900 x 30 metres runway was ready. The work was hindered by an armoured train brought by the Germans to the Cengio (Savona) area, which battered the Vesime zone with its big guns. Luckily for us the fire was random and not well directed. The Allies gave the codename of Excelsior to the new runway.

In September 1944 the partisans had liberated a large area of the Langhe, north-west of Mondovì, between the rivers Tanaro and Bormida. On 10 October the *Autonomi* forced the surrender of the Fascist garrison in the hill town of Alba, now best known for its annual white truffle fair. Garibaldi and Justice and Liberty partisans helped the independents to defend the citadel. But on 2 November the enemy counter-attacked in force, crossed the Tanaro River and re-occupied the town.

Mopping up operations continued in the rest of the liberated zone. The German 34th Division and Republican units engaged the partisans along the banks of the river, drawn there by two daylight airdrops of multicoloured parachutes on 11 and 12 November.

At the height of the fighting, 'Major Temple' was killed as a result of a tragic accident on the 15th. He was aged 31. The CLN of Piedmont paid tribute to the agent in a special order of the day addressed to all partisan groups. General Pensa recalled: 'We had lost a brave officer and a great friend.'

The next day, 'Major Mauri' made a personal call for help to the head of SOE in Italy, Commander Gerard Holdsworth in Monopoli. He relayed the request to Major Macintosh at forward headquarters (TAC HQ) near Florence. As General Pensa recalled, a special flight was then ordered to check on the safety and viability of the new airfield.

At 8.30pm on 17 November a single-engined Westland Lysander army support aircraft landed successfully on Excelsior. The plane left fully laden for the south with a wounded man and two members of a British mission on board. The pilot reported that the Germans had sent in Tiger tanks. A colonel in command of one of the attacking regiments had been killed in desperate fighting.

Early on the morning of 19 November, a B-25 Mitchell bomber and eight P-47 Thunderbolt fighters took off for Vesime from the 12th USAAF's base near Florence. The aim of Operation Blanche was to insert new agents and evacuate other personnel including downed airmen and escaped prisoners of war.

The Mitchell was flown by a Texan lieutenant colonel. He was accompanied by the Lysander pilot. His role was to locate the tanks so that they could be attacked by six of the Thunderbolts.

The planes reached the airfield without incident. The general related that the bomber brought Lieutenant Colonel John Stevens to act as co-ordinator of the various British missions, Captain Hugo Ballard, the radio operator Occaso (Tullio Biondo), and a Major McDonald who left to head another operation.

When the aircraft taxied to the take-off position and the colonel opened the door, he was faced by more than 30 people waiting to board. At the time the enemy was engaging partisans on the perimeter of the field. The pilot finally admitted the maximum number of passengers he could pack into the aircraft - 13 - and took off, a dangerous manoeuvre in the circumstances. Those on board, according to the general, included the crew of two American bombers hit by flack and saved by the partisans, British agents, Lieutenant Giacomino Murgia who was on an assignment to the south, and a Polish informer.

When he was safely back in Florence, the pilot told Major Macintosh what had happened:

It was hell. The ground was soft from the rains and I didn't think the old kite would make it over the hill at the other end. We slowly picked up speed and I could not try and take her off until the very end. I pulled the stick back and she came off the ground shuddering and about to stall. Luckily, we just cleared the hill and I rammed the stick forward to pick up some speed, nearly hit the trees, pulled back once more as we shaved them. Then we were away.

The co-pilot added that as the aircraft cleared the trees his colleague had said: 'Thank you, God. I'll take over now.' [2]

In one of the longest defensive stands in the history of the Resistance, the partisans held out against the enemy for over 40 days until forced to withdraw on 20 December. General Pensa recalled:

The activity of the Excelsior airport came to an abrupt halt on 20 November. The enemy's mopping up operations continued along the Bormida Valley. After having resisted on prepared positions, our forces dispersed into the neighbouring areas, apart from one detachment of chosen men who led guerrilla actions throughout December and into January 1945.

The enemy immediately made the runway unfit for use by ploughing it up. But in January 'Commandant Mauri' arranged for some airdrops to be made on the field, while the 2nd Division of 'Poli' undertook to organise its defence.

On 12 February Republican units pushed into the Bormida Valley with a roundup that lasted about a week. After a fierce battle near the field of Vesime at the Perletto Bridge, 16 partisans of the independent Savona Brigade and the 102nd Garibaldi, led by Lieutenant Bambù (Placido Faro, posthumously awarded the Silver Medal for Military Valour), lay dead on the ground.

Once we had regained control of the area, the runway was remade and extended to a length of 1,100 x 30 metres, thereby making it possible for even the multi-engined transport aircraft to land and take off.

At the beginning of March a Lysander came to collect Lieutenant Colonel Stevens, while bringing Pilot Officer Giacomino Murgia back to us. At the end of the month another Lysander landed to check that the strip was still operational.

On 1 April an American twin-engined Douglas C-47 Dakota transporter landed carrying Lieutenant Colonel Stevens and several other Allied officers. The same aircraft was used to evacuate five seriously wounded personnel, members of several Allied missions who had worked in Piedmont, and the crews of American aircraft who had been saved by our partisans from being captured. Among others, the independents of 'Marcellin' in the Val Chisone brought us 10 men from an American four-engined aircraft that had been obliged to crash land on a field in Airasca and which had then been set on fire the following day by Allied fighters.

On 3 April two C-47s brought 30 British paratroops of the 2nd SAS Regiment to the field, led by Captain [Buck] Macdonald, plus three Polish officers of the ELF Mission, Saganowski, Kowalski and Bogowski, with orders to try to persuade their fellow countrymen enlisted in the *Wehrmacht* to desert.

The last landing was a Lysander on 14 March 1945. It was carrying two British military photographers, Sergeant CJ Dawson and JC Jessiman of the 1st Cinematographic Section. On the return journey the aircraft took three wounded partisans to be treated in liberated territory.

In the final offensive, the *Autonomi* of 'Major Mauri' were the first to take control of the communes of Ceva, Mondoví, Fossano, and to return to Alba. On 27 April the Alpine Divisions entered Turin.

For his contribution to the War of Liberation, Enrico Martini was awarded the Italian Gold Medal for Military Valour, the American Bronze Star, and the Polish Gold Cross. [3] The Commune of Alba was honoured with the Italian Gold Medal for Military Valour for partisan activity. Commander Piero Balbo of the Second Langhe Division, who organised the construction and defence of the partisan airfield at Vesime, was awarded the Italian Silver Medal for Military Valour.

* * *

The Allied airlift to the Italian partisans was achieved by no more than four special duty squadrons and a varying number of bombers and transports diverted from their usual roles.

After the September 1943 Allied landings in the south, the British and Americans took over Italian airfields and built new ones in the olive groves. The personnel, aircraft and equipment were mainly transferred from North Africa. Secret air missions began from Italy to destinations as far afield as the Balkans, Czechoslovakia and Poland.

One of the South African pilots who flew in the Warsaw Airlift from Italy, and was shot down, Major JL van Eysenn, DFC, recalled:

> Airfields were hastily constructed with PSP (perforated steel plates) being laid to form the runways. In addition to numerous fighter and medium bomber squadrons, 205 Group RAF was established at Foggia under the command of Major General JT Durrant. The group consisted of four wings. Three were from the RAF and equipped with the well-proven Vickers Wellington bombers, affectionately known as the 'Wimpy.' The fourth was No. 2 Wing South African Air Force (SAAF), made up of 31 and 34 squadrons, which was equipped with Consolidated B-24 Liberators. Each of the eight squadrons in the group could make about 10 aircraft available at a time. There were also in Italy about two hundred B-17 Flying Fortresses of USAAF.
>
> The role of 205 group was essentially one of strategic long-range night bombing and it employed the technique of 'saturation' developed by Bomber Command in Britain in which the maximum number of aircraft took part.

In a supply role:

> Each aircraft carried 12 canisters in its bomb racks. The containers were crammed with light machine guns, ammunition, hand-grenades, radio equipment, food and medical supplies, and had parachutes attached to them to slow their rate of fall. [4]

Special operations were led by the multinational squadrons of Number 334 Wing RAF at Brindisi. The RAF supplied numbers 148 and 624 squadrons and the Polish Flight, Number 1586. The wing also had a small flight of Lysanders led by Flight Lieutenant Peter Vaughan-Fowler. Number 624 Squadron was sent back to North Africa in February 1944 for missions into southern France and was disbanded in

September following Allied advances. Some of the crews moved to 148 Squadron. Number 624 Squadron was reformed on 28 December 1944 at Grottaglie for a mine-spotting role in the Adriatic, flying Walrus amphibians. The unit finally disbanded on 30 November 1945.

The main British squadron, Number 148 (motto: Trusty), had been reformed for its special duties role in March 1943 at Gambut in north-eastern Libya. The formation was equipped with Halifaxes, Short Stirlings and eventually Liberators. The aircraft were highly modified, had minimal identification markings and were painted black all over.

William (Bill) Steed was a Flight Mechanic (Engines) with 148 Squadron. He enlisted in 1941. After training in England, Bill embarked on the 'Arundel Castle' on 17 June 1942 for the trip round the Cape. Following service on various North African landing grounds, he was posted to the squadron at Derna in Libya on 4 June 1943. The formation was relocated to Brindisi in Italy on 25 January 1944.

Bill Steed told me:

Our work was out on the 'Flights,' which is the area where the aircraft are dispersed rather than in the hangers. Our job was to do the daily inspections for the serviceability of the aircraft we had been allotted to, and to be available when it took off on missions in case of any last minute snags. As the plane returned we were there to guide it from the runway to its own dispersal spot. Any in-flight problems had to be rectified and the aircraft refuelled.

The serviceability of our Halifax aircraft improved considerably on the transfer of the squadron from North Africa to a more temperate climate, but the mountainous country over which they operated with heavy loads put considerable strain on our Merlin in-line engines. A plane returning on only three engines was not an uncommon sight.

Brindisi had only one runway usable by loaded Halifaxes, and this was susceptible to crosswinds that were the cause of many accidents, particularly on the earlier aircraft with the smaller triangular tail fins.

We were the squadron's dogsbodies and were called upon for any job concerned with the aircraft and the smooth running of the airfield. This could be attending to visiting aircraft or laying out the flare paths for night operations. And if guard duties had to be done, guess who they called on? Us of course.

For all that, the feeling of being a part of the action, having contact with the aircrew on their return from operations and knowing that the plane you serviced had safely brought them home was reward enough.

The Americans had their Dakotas and Liberators on the other side of Brindisi's runway. The former were used on pickup missions to the Balkans and elsewhere. The Americans' cinema was a great draw for us.

We groundcrew were aware of the special operations being carried out. We had to be on hand at take-off and could not but notice the 'Joes' [agents] going on board in addition to the aircrew, although at that time we were unaware of their identities or the targets. I read about them after the war.

Aircrew morale appeared to be high, but I have no doubt that the mission to Warsaw in 1944 could have dented that somewhat in view of the terrible losses being sustained.

The courageous aircrew of 148 and 178 squadrons RAF, 31 and 34 squadrons South African Air Force, and 1586 Polish Special Duties Flight, attempted the impossible and almost succeeded.

Bill Steed was demobbed on 20 September 1946. Number 148 Squadron moved to Egypt in November 1945 and was disbanded on 15 January 1946. It was reformed in November and served in various guises until 1965.

* * *

At 10.30 in the morning on Monday, 3 April 2006, a Remotely Operated Vehicle (ROV) of the British Ministry of Defence began searching the bed of Lake Bolsena in the Province of Viterbo, northern Lazio, relaying images to its parent craft on the surface. The Navy crew were from Plymouth.

The aim was to locate a missing World War II bomber, a B-24 Liberator of the South African Air Force, serial number KH 158, which mysteriously disappeared with its eight-man crew in October 1944.

The search was launched at the request of the daughter of one of the missing crew members, Australian Anne Storm. This followed the discovery of a large object in the lake which divers from Romagna Air Finders thought could be the missing aircraft. This Italian group is dedicated to researching and the recovering missing planes for historical and humanitarian reasons. The enthusiasts had been called in by Harry Shindler, the Italy Star Association Representative in Italy. He reasoned that as there was no trace of the Liberator on land, it might be hidden beneath the waters of the lake after having met adverse weather conditions and falling out of control.

Bolsena is Europe's largest volcanic lake. It is about 40 kilometres east of the Tyrrhenian Sea, which was on the flight path of the bombers before the course was set for the Island of Elba and on to northern Italy.

The search was promoted by the British Embassy in Rome, with the support of the Italian authorities, led by the Prefect of Viterbo, Doctor Alessandro Giacchetti. Director of operations was Commander Sean Steeds, the Naval and Air Attaché at the embassy. Also on hand were the volunteers of the Romagna Air Finders, including the president, Leo Venieri, and former airman Pietro Vallesi.

The hunt was conducted at a depth of 100 metres between the beautiful isles of Bisentina and Martana, near the resort of Capodimonte on the southern shore. The bed of the 114.5 square kilometre lake is very irregular and the waters murky and subject to erratic currents.

Over six decades earlier, at 4.15pm on 12 October 1944, 20 Liberators from 31 and 34 squadrons SAAF had taken off from Celone, one of the Foggia group of airbases. The mission was 'supply dropping in northern Italy' to partisans defending liberated territories.

The weather turned stormy. Only three crews were able to deliver their supplies. Low cloud covered most of the drop zones and some planes were blown off course by high winds. Six of the aircraft failed to return to base. Eventually the remains of five of the bombers were found in various locations across Piedmont, four high in the Alps.

However, nothing more was heard of the remaining Liberator after it left Celone, and no wreckage has ever been found. KH 158 of 31 Squadron was captained by Major Selwyn Urry and had been bound for the 'Morris' drop zone (DZ) in Liguria. The crew was South African, British and Australian, and representatives from all the countries' embassies were present at the search.

Anne Storm's father, Flying Officer Thomas Roberts Millar, age 28, was the sole Royal Australian Air Force crew member. He had enlisted in 1942. After training, the officer was assigned to 104 Squadron RAF at Foggia Main airbase in January 1944. In August he was seconded to 31 Squadron SAAF at Celone as leading squadron bomb aimer. Within days, Flying Officer Millar took part in the Warsaw airlift.

Anne was one-year-old when her father disappeared. She has made it her quest to discover what happened to KH 158 on that tragic night.

Lake Bolsena (Anne Storm).

The search vessels at Capodimonte (Anne Storm).

Local residents spoke of three aircraft resting in Lake Bolsena: American and German wartime bombers and a more recent CH-47C Chinook cargo helicopter.

Anne Storm and her husband, Roy, were the guests of honour at the search. Anne recalls the two emotional days:

> The weather was sunny and balmy and the scenery beautiful. It was a long day, both for the investigating team and the shore-based observers who were awaiting news. Sadly, nothing was discovered, but there was still some optimism and it was agreed to carry out a further search on the Tuesday.
>
> At the end of the second day, however, the cable of the ROV became entangled on the wreck of the helicopter on the lake floor and the search was abruptly halted. I was disappointed that the project had ended so swiftly after all the work and preparation involved, but was also philosophical as often these things come to nothing.
>
> If the plane had been found it would have been declared a war grave and left in the lake. I feel very uneasy about this, but it seems to be official British policy. In this event, we would have liked to erect a memorial plaque at the lakeside, which would be a place for the families of the crew to visit.
>
> I greatly appreciate the time and trouble taken by all those concerned in the search and am grateful to the people of Capodimonte for their hospitality and participation.
>
> Perhaps something will create further interest and one day there will be another search.

NOTES

[1] Michael Lees, *No. 1 Special Force and Italian Resistance*, pp 220-1.
[2] Charles Macintosh, *From Cloak to Dagger*, pp 114-15.
[3] After the war, Enrico Martini added Mauri, his *nome di battaglia* to his surname. He graduated in law and became a leading industrialist. Mauri's memoir, entitled *Partigiani Penne Nere: Boves, Val Maudagna, Val Casotto, le Langhe,* was published in 1968. The main title, in English 'The Partisans of the Black Feathers,' is a reference to the distinctive infantry plume of the *Alpini* hat. The patriot died aged 65 in 1976 as the result of an air crash in Turkey.
[4] Major JL van Eysenn, DFC, 'The Warsaw Airlift,' *The South African Military History Society Journal*, June 1983.

8 SOE and Montefiorino

Allied special operations in Italy required men on the ground to act as a link with the growing resistance movement. Fully-fledged liaison officers arrived in occupied territory in the summer of 1944. Some walked across the lines, others were landed by small naval craft, but most were dropped by parachute.

On 9 June the National Liberation Committee for Northern Italy, the *Comitato di Liberazione Nazionale Alta Italia* or *CLNAI*, created a unified military command, the *Corpo Volontari della Libertà (CVL)*. Resistance leaders were ordered to form subsidiary headquarters in their own provinces, known as the *Comando Unico (CU)*.

The new partisan chain of command brought the need for Allied officers to be attached to the main formations. In theory the officers' role was merely advisory. In practice they became major protagonists in the struggle, not least through their ability to call in airdrops of men and supplies.

In June 1944 Major Vivian Johnston became the first British Liaison Officer (BLO). He was sent to an area of great strategic importance astride the Gothic Line. The principal German defensive position ran from Pisa to Rimini through the Apennines. It was known to the Italians as the Green Line.

The tasks of the Envelope Mission were to coordinate the activities of the partisans with the plans of Allied Armies in Italy (AAI), to establish links with the liberation committees, to arrange airdrops of weapons and supplies, and to supervise arrangements in the event of an enemy withdrawal or surrender. There was a parallel American OSS mission commanded by Staff Sergeant Isenberg. Both teams were soon caught up with Allied plans for the advance.

In the wave of optimism following the liberation of Rome on 4 June 1944, the Allies planned to drop Italian paratroops to assist the partisans. Their joint activity would divert the Germans while an offensive began on the main front in Tuscany.

The airdrop was allocated the codename of Operation Albergo and five hundred men of the 185 Battalion of the Nembo Parachute Division began training in the Brindisi area.

The zone chosen for Operation Albergo was Major Johnston's responsibility, the liberated territory in the Emilian Apennines known subsequently as the Partisan Republic of Montefiorino. Its mountainous territory covered the Modena communes of Montefiorino, Frassinoro,

Polinago and Prignano, and those of Toano, Villa Minozzo and Ligonchio in Reggio Emilia. The territory had a population of 50,000, with around 4,600 of those in its capital of Montefiorino.

Today the commune has half as many residents owing to rural depopulation. The village is dominated by its thirteenth century castle. In wartime it often acted as a garrison for the Fascist militia, and now houses both the Museum of the Republic of Montefiorino and the town hall.

The British and American liaison officers were attached to the partisan divisional headquarters, which after the proclamation of the liberated zone on 18 June was based at Montefiorino.

The movement was directed by Mario Ricci (Armando) and Osvaldo Poppi (Davide), both Communist veterans of the Spanish Civil War. They had unified the mountain partisans and led them in a series of daring actions that cleared the upper Secchia Valley of Fascists.

The partisan chief of staff, Marco Nardi, recalled that, though Major Johnston lacked sufficient practical experience in guerrilla warfare, 'he became something more than a liaison officer and could almost be considered a member of the divisional command. He was very young, of pleasant appearance, extrovert and with a perfect knowledge of the Italian language, full of enthusiasm, and eager to ensure the success of the mission through his actions.'

The creation of the liberated zone attracted many youthful recruits, which at the end of June necessitated the reorganisation of the partisan formation into the *Corpo d'Armata Centro Emilia*, or the Army Corps of Central Emilia. It fielded almost seven thousand men in six divisions, four from Modena and two from Reggio Emilia.

As well as the Garibaldi brigades of 'Armando,' the force included a Russian battalion led by Red Army captain Vladimir Pereladov, two Catholic *Italia* brigades commanded by Ermanno Gorrieri, and a mountain battalion led by a priest known as 'Don Carlo,' whose real name was Don Domenico Orlandini.

SOE was given responsibility for mounting Operation Albergo, with HQ AAI holding a watching brief and affording such assistance as might be required. Detailed planning was delegated to the triumvirate of No. 1 Special Force, the Officer Commanding 185 Nembo Battalion, and Lieutenant Colonel Edris, commander of the United States Army Air Force 62nd Troop Transport Group.

The paratroop commander was ordered by AAI: 'You will seize and dominate the area selected by you in the Val di Taro area and put it in a state of defence as a firm base for your future operations, having particular regard in your selection of the locality to defence against tanks. Operations will continue until our forward troops make contact with you or on receipt of further orders from this HQ.'

The plan entered its active phase on 24 July with the issuing of the top-secret 'Operation Order No. 1 to 185 Battalion Nembo Division.' It was D-Day minus eight:

Forward elements of Allied armies in Italy on 24 July 1944 have advanced to the approximate line Pisa - 12 miles north of Florence. Apart from prisoners of war there are no regular Allied troops within the partisan-controlled territory.

Patriot forces supplied with arms despatched by this HQ and under the command of Major Johnston are in complete control of the area between Highway 63 and the Lugo-Pella road.

Contact with Major Johnston and with other patriot units operating in his area is maintained over four W/T [wireless telegraphy] links. Major Johnston's HQ is in the area of Villa Minozzo.

In addition, the following are also controlled by partisans: a zone 5 miles deep and 10 miles long to the west of Highway 63, and the area within a radius of 10 miles of Bedonia.

Patriot forces under Major Johnston's command total 5,000 lightly armed men, organised as one Garibaldi Corps consisting of two Modena and one [Reggio] Emilian Division.

On the night of 26-27 July an advance party of 10 persons will be delivered to Major Johnston in order to prepare reception for 185 Battalion. The group will consist of one officer from the battalion, four British officers and a W/T operator, and four Italian signalmen from 185 Battalion. Captain Holland will be in command of this advance party.

The area within which 185 Battalion Nembo will operate is suitable for guerrilla warfare. It is bounded by two main roads, Reggio Emilia to Spezia, and Modena to Lucca, which the enemy is attempting to keep open.

With only light weapons at their disposal the patriots have been able to deny vast areas to the enemy. With the increase in firepower and trained troops, which 185 Battalion will provide, it will be possible to extend the area controlled by the partisans to cover the main roads in addition to the mountain heights.

The patriot forces astride the enemy lines of communication in the Apennines form an integral part of military operations to be carried out by the Allied armies in the immediate future.

Enemy forces south of the River Po are impeded in the rear by the destruction of all bridges across the Po and their forward elements are engaged by the Allied armies between Livorno and Ancona.

The mountainous area between the Po and the Allied armies therefore assumes importance for the enemy in that he must endeavour -

(1) To keep his lines of communication clear for the transport of material to his forward units, and:
(2) To prepare for a withdrawal northward to the Po or westward into Liguria in the event of a defeat on the main Italian front.

185 Battalion Nembo Division will cooperate with partisans in the Spezia area in carrying out guerrilla warfare against the enemy. [1]

On 15 July Special Force base signalled to Major Johnston that the paratroops had completed their training, and asked: 'Can you receive the Battalion, when can it be dropped and what effect would the operation have on local partisans?' He replied on the 18th: 'Parachute battalion project excellent providing the drop is by night and maximum supplies are received. Can arrange night reception at Prati di Sara. Eureka required.'

Eureka was the radio-beacon location system, which allowed an aircraft to home in to a ground position.

An outline of the operation was sent to the major on 21 July together with the instruction that the DZ was to be known as Barr. Stores and heavy weapons would be delivered before the paratroops were dropped.

The officer changed the location next day, keeping the same codename, saying that Frassinoro would be more suitable to receive the battalion. The village is only 11 kilometres south-west of Montefiorino.

On 25 July base signalled: 'Confirmation that advance party will arrive on 26-27 July,' and next day sent details of the group and the expected time on target.

The order to the Nembo Battalion included the arrangements for delivery to the field:

The battalion will be dropped to a reception prepared by British liaison officers and Italian patriots. The force will enplane in 42 aircraft of 62 Group at Brindisi Airfield at 11.00 hours local time on 1 August 1944 or at the same time and place on the first suitable day after that date. Additional equipment will be carried by 12 Halifax aircraft of 334 Wing and will be delivered to Major Johnston's reception before 1 August 1944. There it will be stored awaiting 185 Battalion's arrival.

Aircraft of 62 Group will depart from Brindisi at 12.00 hours on 1 August 1944 and will stage at Gallera Airfield, Rome, and take off again at dusk and fly to the pinpoint...

On reaching the ground, 185 Battalion Nembo Division will immediately consolidate and the Officer Commanding will place himself under the orders of Major VR Johnston who will be there to receive him. The major is the direct representative of AAI, through this HQ, in the Spezia area. [2]

Communication by wireless telegraphy with HQ and within Emilia would be arranged by Captain Holland of the Royal Corps of Signals, who would drop with the advance party. Midget receiving sets would also be delivered in case special messages needed to be broadcast over the BBC or Radio Bari. In addition, couriers could be sent across the lines, and pigeon lofts delivered to the field if required.

Six Wellington bombers from numbers 142 and 150 squadrons of 340 Wing RAF were added to the Halifaxes of Number 148 Squadron assigned to the airlifting of supplies. The Wellingtons could only carry six containers each, but the supplies were urgently needed.

A directive to Major Johnston on 27 July spelt out his tasks:

Receive battalion and consolidate in dropping area. Carry out such raids on German transport, troops, vital points and lines of communication as are possible without becoming involved in a pitched battle. Build up a strong partisan force around the battalion to be used in strength (possibly openly) against the enemy when he begins to withdraw. At all times ensure firm base and safe W/T communications. Further orders will be passed by W/T in accordance with the requirements of the military situation. [3]

Two parties were dropped by the Americans of the OSS Detachment with the 8th Army. Their wireless operators were codenamed Gigi and Pia.

The first message from 'Pia' was on 25 July. It said: 'All well. Not dropped in our area. Are in the province of Reggio Emilia.' At eight next morning 'Gigi' reported they were near Villa Minozzo with the Sixth Garibaldi Brigade and that the area was completely clear of Germans. Base noted the party had been dropped about 30 miles west of target. They were in Reggio Emilia not Modena province.

In the afternoon 'Pia' signalled: 'Contacted British major [Johnston] who has radio in Villa Minozzo. Will start moving towards our area tomorrow.'

The next message from 'Pia' was on 29 July. He said:

We are in contact with a force of 10,000 partisans who request the following weapons and medical supplies: Bazookas with ammunition - 81mm mortars with ammunition in belts - Sten guns - Bren and Breda machine guns - anti-tank mines - anti-personnel mines - gasoline and money for them. If you want, ask for explanation. Medicine for external wounds - adhesive - gauze compresses - denatured alcohol - tincture of iodine - First Aid packets and equipment - disinfecting liquids - stretchers - cotton - drugs and dressings.

The wireless operator was asked to confirm the number of partisans.

At eight next morning 'Gigi' requested detailed maps of the area, but by three in the afternoon 'Pia' was signalling: 'Sixty German motorised transport in Castel Nuovo nei Monti to support an attack against partisans defending Villa Minozzo. I believe our request complete. Number of partisans exact.'

The operator was told to pinpoint his location more exactly in future. He replied immediately:

'Requested explanation tomorrow. Germans attacking our positions. Situation critical. Urge intervention Air Force at Sassuolo, where there are about 150 German tanks and a strong concentration of Germans. About 5,000. At Levizzano, Castelvecchio and Lorignino sulla Secchia. Confirm intervention Air Force.'

The party was told to move to Verga and an aerial reconnaissance was ordered.

A message from 'Gigi' five hours later said: 'Villa Minozzo occupied by the Germans. Suggest bombing. Suspend dropping material in zone.'

At 8.30 in the morning of 31 July he reported: 'We are at Montefiorino, near the Partisans' Army HQ, commanding officer Armando. Strength: 10,000 men including Allied ex-prisoners of war, and 30 trucks and 300 horses. Tuscan partisans seek to unite with this army. By helping the Sixth Brigade we will be supplied with passes and men to help us reach our zone and work.' The party was now ordered to make for Vergato in the Province of Bologna.

Two and a half hours later 'Pia' signalled: 'Since midnight last night we have been sustaining strong attacks with artillery. Surrounded on all sides. Our positions holding. We are trying to disengage towards Tuscany, where the partisan army intends to operate behind the Gothic Line. Urge energetic air intervention at Villa Minozzo, Sassuolo, Pievepelago and Lama Mocogno. We are surrounded. We are waiting. Send us orders.'

AAI HQ was informed and an immediate aerial armed reconnaissance ordered. By 10 in the evening, Air Support Control reported by telephone that 22 Spitfires had hit the four targets. Some anti-aircraft fire had been encountered at Lama Mocogno and Pievepelago. The centre added: 'Spitfires go out again tomorrow morning.'

There was no confirmation of the messages from Major Johnston and there was much speculation at Allied HQ as to whether the Germans had captured the wireless operators and were using their sets.

Meanwhile, Halifax bombers of 148 Squadron RAF had dropped the Anglo-Italian advance party to DZ Barr at Frassinoro on the night of 26-27 July in Operation Batepits. The commander, Captain Charles Holland, was aged 26. He was accompanied by three other experienced SOE agents: captains James (Jim) Thomas Mann Davies, Royal Engineers, who was 30, Ernest Hulton Wilcockson, Royal Artillery, aged 27, and Lloyd-Roberts, Royal Army Medical Corps. He was injured during the drop. The British wireless operators were corporals Frank Hayhurst and Frank Barrett.

Jim Davies recalled:

Johnston was a fluent Italian speaker. He'd been dropped into Montefiorino because of the Armando controlled area, and he was to report on the efficacy of the Republic as a base for military operations. He thought that it could be built up into quite a useful force which could be a thorn in the side of the Germans and Fascists.

This was a very hurried operation, like a lot of wartime opportunities. I didn't even see or work with the Nembo Division at all. I don't suppose any of us did. Quite clearly, if there was going to be a surprise attack in the opening phase it was going to be very difficult, particularly if the 5th Army attack did not succeed.

The bad news started to come in the day after we dropped. We knew that the Fascists were on the move. The news had come via partisan outposts. There was a lot of rumour and fear, not only amongst the partisans but also the villagers too. Charles and I were a little bit sceptical to start with that all this was serious, but then Johnston was convinced that it was going to be very rough. There had been a heavy drop of supplies with our advance party, which confirmed to the enemy their worst fears about Montefiorino. [4]

On 1 August Captain Irving-Bell at Special Force base reported to the American colonel in charge of Special Operations at AAI, John Riepe:

The following has been received from the area:

Holland, Wilcockson, Roberts, Everitt and all W/T operators with Envelope at Ravina. Davies and Faccione are at Frassinoro. Johnston was last reported at Villa Minozzo, therefore it is impossible to obtain his or the partisan moves at present.

Report of Hun moves today. Down road from Sassuolo as far as Ceredolo. Reported but not confirmed that the Germans have reached Montefiorino. Down road from fork to Minozzo and Villa Minozzo. Here guns have been shelling villages southwards. From Pievepelago east along road to fork and then north towards Piandelagotti. Targets to bomb are Sassuolo road as far as Ceredolo and the road at Pievepelago. Can accept no drop yet.

We have answered as follows:

Very sorry indeed to receive such bad news. Nembo standing by ready to take off on the night of 1-2 August. Unfortunately, this is the only time at which RAF will be able to carry out operations. The decision must rest with you. We can still drop Nembo if you can organise reception on Barr.

90

You must also decide whether they can fulfil a useful function at this stage. They are an excellent body of men and despite lack of heavy weapons will still be able to give a good account of themselves. However, you must be able to assure them safe reception and at least four hours safety in which to get organised. Reply on the same [wireless] sched[ule]. Keep smiling and let us know your requirements in bombing small arms stores.

The message to the colonel closed with: 'Imperative bomb the following targets: bridges at Sassuolo and Gatta, all roads from Villa Minozzo to road fork, and from Pievepelago to Piandelagotti.'

A force of about 8,000 Germans armed with artillery, armoured cars and flame-throwers carried out a three-pronged attack on the liberated zone. The Fascists secured the means of communication. Allied agents joined the partisans in scrambling to avoid encirclement and Operation Albergo was hastily cancelled.

The bulk of the partisan force escaped to the upper Panaro Valley or to Tuscany. The corps divided into its constituent parts.

The Reggio Emilia partisans formed a *Comando Unico*, a Green Flame brigade and a mountain battalion.

The Modena fighters moved into the Bologna Apennines under the leadership of 'Armando' and on 29 September crossed into Allied-held territory. Refusing to accept the demobilisation usually meted out to irregular forces in such circumstances, the Modena Armando Division was incorporated into the 5th Army's battle line and fought alongside the regulars until the end of the war.

'Armando,' Mario Ricci, was awarded the Italian Gold Medal for Military Valour in 1953. So too was the little commune of Montefiorino in 1971.

There are two conflicting theories about the failure of Operation Albergo: that the timing of the enemy offensive against the partisans, which ruined the whole enterprise, was just an unfortunate coincidence, or that the action was intelligence-led.

There were spies everywhere and local commanders may certainly have responded to reports of the arrival of agents and supplies by parachute. However, a few weeks earlier the Germans had been so concerned about the build up of the rebel force on their flank that their General Messerle had proposed a truce. It had been rejected by the partisans. They replied: 'We came to the mountains to fight, not to withdraw from the struggle.' The massive German and Fascist attack was most likely their response to this rebuff.

The commander of the advance party, Charles Holland, later expressed doubts on the viability of the project:

Our target, agreed upon by both the 5th Army Command and No. 1 Special Force, was to plan and prepare the logistical, organisational and military aspects of the drop of a parachute battalion of the Nembo Division behind the German line in the Tuscan-Emilian Apennines.

This operation should have taken place at the end of July during the full moon period and was meant as a diversion to disturb the enemy just when the 5th Army intended to advance on Lucca. The plan was based on an optimistic, too much so, perhaps, as it later appeared, evaluation of the strength and quality of the partisan forces operating in the area and also on the fact that the 5th Army Command was convinced that they would soon definitely break the Gothic Line. Actually, the situation we found did not allow for any hope of success. [5]

Jim Davies added:

Within three days of our arrival, the Germans launched counter-measures which disrupted the whole operation, and the advance party had to scatter. Elements of the Hermann Goering Division, in the process of its long-delayed withdrawal from the Italian theatre, made a thorough and rapid drive against the Resistance in the Modena and Reggio mountains, assisted by other German troops, the militia, and the *Decima Mas* of Prince Valerio Borghese which carried out a wider sweep lasting for more than three weeks.

Had the enemy received prior intelligence, as has been suggested, then surely he would have held his fire until the whole parachute battalion had been dropped before launching a heavy mopping up operation?

Charles Holland, who had been a fellow officer in Greece, and I teamed up with Corporal Hayhurst. Owing to the severity of the *rastrellamento* we had difficulty in obtaining food, and naturally we slept out of doors at night. [6]

In a wartime report, made on re-crossing the lines, Jim Davies provided more information on the escape from the enemy:

On advice from Base, Johnston's mission was advised to join Major Lett at Zeri in south Liguria. We divided up into four parties. Apart from one set for Johnston, the remainder of the W/T stores was buried.

All parties set out at night and avoided the enemy encircling movement. After five days, I met two partisans with the news that the enemy was already occupying the Zeri area. After going back to inform Johnston and Wilcockson who were on Monte Tondo, I set up quarters with a local band above Comano and there I met Holland's party including the two W/T operators. We decided Charles should return and collect a buried W/T set and at the same time take an operator back for Wilcockson.

Our plan was that we should set up a station, pass intelligence and arrange for drops that would enable us to arm the bands then reorganising in western Reggio and Parma and near Comano. After the set had made contact, I set off on 26 August to reconnoitre the Spezia-Parma road as our idea was to start activity by interrupting the free flow of enemy communications.

Drops failed to materialise, but resistance was hardening as partisans got better organised and the prospect of an Allied advance became real. At the end of August, the Justice and Liberty Brigade repelled three armoured cars and two trucks of troops which attempted to open up the Parma Valley again. We passed on to bands instructions for operations on D-Day and then received a directive to contact Parma CLN and to have liaison with it in case of enemy withdrawal.

We moved our joint mission, composed of Captain Holland, myself, then also a captain, and Corporal Hayhurst with the W/T set, right down into Parma Province and established close contact with the partisan bands at the beginning of September. [7]

The Italian members of the advance party were able to cross the lines. They were accompanied by Allied escaped prisoners of war and downed airmen, though some of the others caught in the enemy drive were summarily executed.

Jim Davies recalled subsequent events:

The strong partisan formations defending the Montefiorino box, and one parachute battalion, all immobile, could not have held out unless the 5th Army was to break through and this could only happen in the unlikely event of a German withdrawal.

Neither were the strength and effectiveness of the enemy reaction foreseen. Of course, this is all in hindsight.

The principal spin-off of the abortive Batepits operation was the transformation of some members of the advance party - Wilcockson, Holland and myself - into Liaison Officers. Our job was to re-establish contact with those Resistance leaders who had survived the widespread drives of August and to help in reforming scattered units on a reduced basis, for the difficulties were now clearly appreciated and no major advance was expected in the western Apennines. At the same time, the problem of maintaining formations under the changed weather conditions of winter had to be considered. From time to time, our dropping zones in Parma were raided by night-flying Fieseler Storch, without serious effect, and there were also sudden drives. So precautions had to be taken, but none of these attacks were organised on the scale of those in August, except for the local raid on the Parma *Comando Unico*. Villagers were now much less shaken by these raids and always supported us loyally.

In October 1944 Charles Holland and I, together with Hayhurst the W/T operator, were quartered in Grammatica in the Parma Apennines, whilst the *Comando Unico*, with whom we were then in daily contact, was stationed nearby in Bosco di Corniglio. Early one morning, we heard firing from the direction of Bosco and soon messengers told us the village was surrounded by Germans. We immediately packed our W/T set and baggage on mules and set off up the valley to Riana. Next day we were told exactly what had happened.

The German garrison and militia from Berceto on the Cisa road, Route 62, had surrounded and raided Bosco. They had captured and shot Pablo [Giacomo di Crollanza], the *Comandante,* and after tying him down had burnt alive in his bed a recently arrived emissary of the CLNAI Milan. Both were Communists. In fact the raid was characterised equally by brutality and ineptitude as, had the enemy arrived early in darkness, they could have closed all escape routes and captured the entire *Comando Unico*.

Later, HQ decided that I should cross the lines, which I did in November. It thus fell to Major Holland to help rebuild the Parma *Comando Unico* and partisan organisation and arrange supplies, even though the DZs continued to be raided by the enemy. [8]

Ernest Wilcockson recalled the final phase of the war in the mountains:

It was obvious that the partisans were not able to mount a serious attack on the German force and that their main needs were arms, clothing and so on. Unfortunately the mission and the area had a low priority, so supply drops, which had to be made at night, were few and far between.

The main task then became the collection of information concerning enemy movements and much valuable intelligence gathered by the partisans was passed on to No. 1 Special Force HQ. We also managed to collect some Allied airmen who had been shot down, together with a few escaped POWs who had made their way into the mountains.

As the winter of 1944 approached, it became obvious that the Allies would not be able to break through to the Po Valley and we received instructions to damp down partisan activities until the spring. This caused much distress and disappointment to the partisans, who were now faced with a winter in the mountains.

The Allied air forces had taken control of the air, and daylight drops became possible. From our original single plane at night, we began to receive drops by three or more at once. This enabled us to start a build-up of arms and ammunition for the following spring.

Meanwhile, the partisan units had become much more organised and ready to assist the Allies when the time came for the breakout. I think it would be safe to say that, despite the occasional *rastrellamento* or sweep by the enemy, the partisans were now in control of the mountain area.

At the beginning of January 1945, Mike Lees and Bert Farrimond, his radio operator, were dropped in and moved over to the Secchio-Febbio area. In early February, Jim Davies and John Stott arrived to take over the Silentia Mission, when Charles Barratt and I returned to our advance HQ in Florence.

I will always remember the time I spent in the mountains, the kindness shown by the ordinary people and the friendships formed. It was an honour to have served among them. [9]

* * *

In the wake of the failure of Operation Albergo and the fall of the Partisan Republic of Montefiorino, the Apennines unexpectedly came to provide a base for SOE activity until the liberation.

Major Johnston remained in the mountains till early January 1945 with the Envelope Mission to the Reggio Emilia partisans. Major Ernest Wilcockson took over the eastern sector in the Silentia Mission in Modena. His wireless operator was Charles Barratt. The mission originally run jointly by Jim Davies and Charles Holland was codenamed Toffee or Envelope Blue and covered the East Cisa area in Parma Province. Their signalmen were Frank Hayhurst and Frank Barrett.

In late October 1944 a Tactical Headquarters (TAC HQ) was also established, in a villa on the high road between Florence and Fiesole, to liase between No. 1 Special Force and 5th Army Headquarters. Under the command of Major Charles Macintosh, DSO, the forward headquarters assumed operational control of all British and Italian missions within the tactical area, including responsibility for signals, supplies, courier services and intelligence.

The presence of a network of No. 1 Special Force missions, together with a local headquarters near Florence, sustained and encouraged Resistance activity. One of the most daring enterprises was a British plot to kill or capture a German general - the topic of the next chapter.

NOTES

[1] 'Operation Order No. 1 to 185 Battalion Nembo Division,' TNA: PRO WO 204/7304.

[2] Ibid.

[3] Ibid.

[4] Laurence Lewis, *Echoes of Resistance*, pp 56-7.

[5] Charles Holland, 'Toffee: A British Mission to the East Cisa Area (1944-1945),' *No. 1 Special Force and Italian Resistance*, p 271.

[6] Jim Davies, 'Two Missions to the Apennines,' *No. 1 Special Force and Italian Resistance*, pp 229-30.

[7] 'Report on the Parma Mission for August, September and October 1944,' by Major JTM Davies, RE, TNA: PRO HS 6/844.

[8] Jim Davies, 'Two Missions to the Apennines,' *No. 1 Special Force and Italian Resistance*, pp 231-2.

[9] Ernest Wilcockson, 'With the Partisans of the Modena Area,' *No. 1 Special Force and Italian Resistance*, pp 243-4.

9 Target: General 'X'

In the autumn of 1944 No. 1 Special Force planned to remove a notorious German general from the scene. SOE agents in Tuscany and Emilia had reported to the base in Monopoli that forces under his command had carried out widespread reprisals against civilians.

The chosen enforcer was Major John Barton, a young commando who had already been awarded the DSO and MC for leadership and gallantry in action behind the lines in Italy. This is his top-secret wartime account of the operation, which was codenamed Cisco Red:

My task was to kill or capture General 'X,' whose HQ was reported to be at 'Y.'

I left Brindisi on the night of 3 November in a Liberator bomber together with stores for Silentia and two Italians, a captain and a private. They had orders to proceed to Bologna and set up a radio station.

We arrived over the target area at 22.00 hours. The pilot saw the fires some distance away and on the first run in dropped his containers. He did not know how many fires there should have been but took it for granted that everything was in order. He made one circuit and then we jumped in the order: myself, the captain and the private.

It was a bright moonlit night and it took us four and a half minutes to reach the ground, so we must have baled out at about 3,000 feet. We landed very near the fires and immediately Wilcockson came up and said that it had been a first class drop. Some of the containers had actually landed amongst the fires. All the holders except one were found and taken to a neighbouring farmhouse. The missing container was later reported to have stuck to the plane.

I remained that night and the next day at Wilcockson's HQ, a very comfortable house in Gova. He was annoyed because I had not brought him any mail or money. He was pleased with the contents of the drop, although it contained no clothing or boots, which he badly needed. We couldn't understand why the containers had all been padded with hundreds of useless sandbags instead of something like greatcoats or socks. Some partisans stole one container and its contents but we eventually recovered it intact. The Italians left for Bologna - the captain did not appear to be very happy.

The following day we rode over to Johnston's mission at Ligonchio and discussed my task. He said I would have to wait several days for a guide, so I stayed with him. As I could not speak Italian or German I decided to form a small squad to take with me. I finally left with an ex-POW as interpreter, an Italian parachutist who had a good reputation amongst the partisans, and a German-Italian who said he could pass as a German.

On the day we left there was a massed daylight drop. It was pathetic! The planes released their containers from 5,000-6,000 feet and half the parachutes did not open. Most of the ammunition was ruined. Quite a few containers dropped into enemy hands. As there were no Germans within 36 hours walk, the drop was pretty inaccurate. Wilcockson said he received some ancient Italian rifles and that they were far more dangerous to the users than to their targets.

We marched for three days until we came to the edge of the mountains overlooking Reggio. From this point on we were in German and Fascist controlled territory and it was necessary to move by night. The partisans were very afraid of my British uniform and wanted me to wear civilian clothes, but according to my orders I refused. The German-Italian left me here. Things did not look quite so easy to him as they had done at Ligonchio.

We borrowed bicycles and a guide came up from Reggio to fetch us. We left the mountains at dusk and at 23.00 hours were cycling through Reggio high street. There had been a little transport on the main road, but it was very ancient and slow and made a lot of noise, so it was easy to get into the ditch and watch it pass. The vehicles had no lights. In Reggio a German cyclist patrol came up and asked what we were doing. The guide replied that it was none of their business and we pedalled like madmen through the city. By the time the Germans had got off their bicycles, unslung their rifles or machine pistols and fired, we were out of sight and riding in and out of little side roads. Shooting at night in any big town is quite usual. The Germans fire into the air to give themselves confidence.

We came to the railway station only to find ourselves surrounded by three patrols. They were talking and laughing and making a lot of noise. Fortunately, the Air Force had been over in the day to bomb the station. They had not hit it, but had made a mess of the houses around about, in one of which we hid. There was a train in the station unloading goods and I later found out that it could only travel about 15 kilometres owing to the bridges having been bombed. There were quite a few troops about, but they were all loaded with equipment and obviously in transit. The blackout was very good. The patrols passed and we cycled to a house in the suburbs and had an excellent meal and a good bed.

We stayed in Reggio two or three days. The [partisan] commandant came to see me the first morning and proved both efficient and helpful. He said he would give me a guide to Modena. The Italian parachutist wanted to get into civilian clothes as he was wearing British battledress. The commandant was able to give him good papers, so I consented. That afternoon the soldier went out to see a friend and look around. He was stopped by a patrol. His papers were examined and found to be in order, but he was arrested for carrying an automatic pistol in his hip pocket. Foolish man! We did not see him again.

We left Reggio at about 17.30 hours one night and cycled along the Via Emilia, the main Modena road. I had a silent Sten slung over my shoulder, which made me feel rather conspicuous, but in the half light two groups of German privates took no notice. We passed a horse-drawn convoy about three kilometres long and nearly came to grief when we ran into a bunch of drivers straggling across the road. The bicycles had poor brakes and we could not stop. The drivers swore at us but did nothing else. A motor convoy passed us going towards Modena, but they dared not use lights for fear of an attack. We stopped at a priest's house and changed guides. The new one took us off the main road along narrow paths until we came to the River Secchia. We waded across. Apparently the bridge on the main road had been bombed and now there was only a guarded footbridge. The transport took a detour and crossed the river at a good bridge further north.

We rode into Modena by the side of the railway line and stopped for the night in a house in the main street, next door to a Fascist HQ. The city was very quiet and there were few patrols. We spent the next day peeping through the blinds. The guards examined passes and a few Germans went by. We changed houses every night on foot and our cycles were brought to the new dwelling the next day. We passed two Germans in one street who looked us up and down suspiciously. They had their weapons slung round their necks ready to fire, but I think they must have felt that two against three was not a good thing, so said nothing. Our biggest danger at this time seemed to be the bombing and the strafing by the Air Force - which was sometimes unpleasantly close.

I saw the [partisan] commandant and he provided me with another guide to take us to Mirandola. Unfortunately, the partisans had ambushed a small party of Germans on the road we had hoped to use. The enemy were very busy burning houses, searching everywhere and shooting people. Seventy-five dwellings were raised to the ground. We made a large detour and rode along the bank of the River Secchia until we came to Concordia, which was a known partisan area. We waited several days here while they tried to make contacts further east, but it was very difficult. The Ferrara area was full of spies - Germans and Fascists, in that order. Finally, we made a contact in the Bondeno area and started out, moving a short distance each night, living in holes in walls, under haystacks, in barns and stables, and all manner of peculiar hideouts.

There was a considerable amount of mechanical transport on the Poggio Rusco road, which we sat and watched. The drivers were terrified of the Air Force and as soon as the warning was put up - white flags placed along the road - would hide their vehicles behind houses and trees. For some unknown reason the planes neglected Mirandola, a small Fascist town ringed by trees under which the Germans had concealed petrol, food, ammunition and a very large number of vehicles. When I left the area most of this material had been moved.

There was a large factory on the road leading east from Mirandola. Here the Germans collected all the sugar beet from the farmers, without payment, and from it produced raw alcohol in considerable quantities. This was taken away daily to the north of the Po in horse-drawn vehicles.

The partisans were well informed of all German billets in this area and could not understand why they were not bombed. There was a meat producing plant in the town where all the cattle and pigs were slaughtered, tinned and sent to Germany. A small train in the Cavezzo area took men to and from work. This was continually being strafed although the Germans did not use it. Sometimes they would run a goods train behind it as a cover but not often.

The next month was spent in the Bondeno-Ferrara area. Life was possible but unpleasant. The whole district was being continually searched and pillaged. The few partisans had a very thin time living in their holes. Many were captured and shot immediately. There was a spy in the Ferrara band and they were practically all taken by the Fascists.

I finally contacted the acting Ferrara [partisan] commandant and told him the information I required. We interrogated German prisoners, deserters, Russians and Poles, and partisans in all the villages. In fact we tried every channel that was open to us, but there was no clue as to the general's whereabouts. There was a large HQ south of Ferrara with a general living there, but he commanded the district and was not my man at all. One report said that General 'X' was now on the western front, but there was nothing to confirm this. Strangely enough, everyone seemed to know where Kesselring was - one week at Sassuolo, the next at Ferrara, then possibly Verona or Venice, and so on. All the larger commands change their HQs very frequently to guard against bombing attacks.

We made one very good contact, which might have produced results but for the untimely interference of the Fascists. We stayed at the house of a captain of militia who was a good Fascist by day and an even better partisan by night. He commanded a considerable area north of the Po and was friendly with many useful Germans. He ran trucks from Verona to the Bondeno area. One way he carried arms for the partisans, and the other, goods for the Germans. He seemed fairly sure that General 'X' was not south of the Po but probably somewhere in the Verona-Brescia area. The captain agreed to go to Verona and find out for sure.

The day after he left, we were peeping through the shutters of our hiding place, a small room, when three trucks of Fascist troops came along the road. We decided that it was a good thing to be on the safe side, so jumped out of the window and hid amongst the sugar beet in the field outside. It was fortunate that we did, for the troops first surrounded the house and then searched it from top to bottom and so began a very thorough comb out of the area.

There was obviously a spy at work for the Fascists went to all the partisans' houses, found weapons and explosives, and took them all prisoner. The search went on for several days, during which time we lived in the open fields and begged for food from women and children. Finally, the Germans took over and went around asking: 'Where are the Englishmen?' They burned the house we had stayed in, so somebody [had] talked.

While this was going on my interpreter walked out, so I had to learn to speak Italian very rapidly. When things cooled down again I found that all my partisan contacts had been taken or shot. I stayed in the area for another 10 days, wandering from house to house, trying to pick up the partisans again, but with little success. Most people thought I was a spy as everywhere we had been the Germans had followed. To make matters worse, I was lousy and had caught scabies some time ago.

Just before Christmas, I decided that General 'X' was definitely not south of the Po and so the answer was to cross and try the Verona-Venice area. I made my way back to Concordia and bribed an Italian to take me to the partisans. He did. It is not difficult to cross the Po - the partisans said they would smuggle me across in the back of a truck or better still row me across in a boat.

Before leaving, I sent for the [partisan] commandant of the Modena area and asked him to send messages to Milan, Verona, Venice and all the big cities in the north to find out where my man was. He agreed to do this, but said that he could not give me the information required in under five or six weeks owing to the difficulty of movement. I told him to carry on.

In the meantime I decided to return to base to find out if any more definite information could be given me there, and, what I considered equally important, to report on the situation of the partisans in the plains.

An American sergeant gunner had baled out in the area a few days before and had joined the partisans, so I took him with me and left for the mountains on 27 December. I was in a hurry to get back and felt depressed at the failure of my mission. I borrowed an Italian soldier's cape and with that thrown over my shoulders we set out by day for the Sassuolo area and so into the mountains. The American was dressed in civilian clothes. I reached Wilcockson at Gova on the 29th. The airman I had to leave with the partisans at the base of the mountains, as his feet were bad.

The journey was quite uneventful. The few Germans we passed did not even glance twice. Along the Via Gardenia leading to Sassuolo there were any number working along the side of the road digging trenches. I was watching them and not the road, with the unfortunate result that I fell off my bike in front of them - they laughed!

There was the normal garrison of about 250 Germans in Sassuolo, but we bypassed the town and entered the mountains a little to the south. We left our bicycles and in about six inches of snow started walking. At a place called Monchio I found the Italian captain and the private who had come with me into the area. On their way to Bologna they had been fired at, so had thought it better to return to the mountains!

At Gova, Wilcockson was in good form, surrounded by parachutes, containers and weapons. Despite all his drops he still needed clothing and medical supplies very badly. I waited two days for the American to catch me up, but as he did not arrive I left on 1 January with a South African fighter pilot who had been shot down in the plains three months before.

From Gova to Catigliano, where we contacted the first American patrol, it took us 47 hours march, with few halts and little to eat. Unfortunately for us the line had changed a few days before, so that when we arrived at Civago it was difficult to find a guide to take us. When we did, he was so scared that he made a big detour and took us by a shocking route. With us were some 20 civilians.

We saw no Germans at all, but it was hardly to be expected - none would be foolish enough to take the route we did. We had slight difficulty in finding the Americans, but when we did they made us very welcome. Nobody questioned my word that I was who I said I was or asked for my papers. We had reached the Americans at about 18.00 hours, so we stayed with them that night and the following day. They gave us transport into Florence. From there I flew to Naples and then on to base. [1]

Lieutenant Colonel Richard Hewitt - new Commanding Officer of No. 1 Special Force - circulated Major Barton's report on 13 January 1945 with the order that it should 'on no account receive a wider distribution.'

A 'secret and personal' copy sent next day by Major de Haan to Lieutenant Colonel Pleydell-Bouverie at Special Operations Mediterranean (SOM), Liaison Staff, Allied Forces Headquarters, was accompanied by this letter:

The enclosed report by Major BJ Barton, DSO, MC, is passed to you personally, as we understand that Field Marshal Alexander was personally interested in the progress of this operation whilst he was at AAI. We kept him advised, through Major Gibson, of any information received from Major Barton whilst he was in the field.

We should be most grateful if you have the opportunity to pass this report on to Field Marshal Alexander. If not, please retain it for your personal files.

John Barton made clear in his report that he was not seeking the German Commander-in-Chief in Italy, Field Marshal Albert Kesselring. The major's boss, Charles Macintosh, DSO, provided a possible clue as to the reason for this in his memoir *From Cloak to Dagger:*

> At TAC HQ we had often discussed the possibility of capturing or killing Kesselring. I cannot vouch for the accuracy of the report but was told that Alexander on hearing of the idea had exclaimed:
>
> 'Nothing doing. If they get Kesselring a new man will take his place and I'll have to work out anew his reaction to any situation. Leave him alone.' [2]

Field Marshal Alexander intervened again on the German commander's behalf when the British sentenced him to death in 1947. Albert Kesselring was captured by American troops on 6 May 1945 and tried for War Crimes by a British Military Court in Venice in 1947. He was charged with being concerned in the killing of some 335 Italian nationals in the Ardeatine Caves in Rome on 24 March 1944 and with inciting and commanding his forces to kill Italian civilians as reprisals.

For most of the last 12 months of the war the Field Marshal had been in charge of anti-partisan warfare. On 1 May 1944 Field Marshal Keitel, as Commander-in-Chief of all German Forces, gave Kesselring the overall command and direction in the fight against Italian partisans, who had become a serious menace to the security of the German Forces. For this purpose all SS and police forces in Italy, as well as the fighting services, were brought under his command.

On 17 June Field Marshal Kesselring issued new regulations for partisan warfare, which included the wording: 'The fight against the partisans must be carried out with all means at our disposal and with the utmost severity. I will protect any commander who exceeds our usual restraint in the choice and severity of the means he adopts whilst fighting partisans ... partisans must be attacked and destroyed.'

A further directive on 1 July stated: 'Where there are considerable numbers of partisan groups a proportion of the male population of the area will be arrested. In the event of acts of violence being committed these men will be shot. The population must be informed of this. Should troops be fired on from any village, the village will be burnt down. Perpetrators or ringleaders will be hanged in public.'

On 21 August the Field Marshal acknowledged that 'instances had occurred within the last few weeks which caused the greatest harm to the dignity and discipline of the German Armed Forces and which had nothing to do with punitive measures.' On 24 September Kesselring added: 'The *Duce* has furnished me with fresh instances which are revolting in the manner in which they have been carried out and are driving even the peaceful elements of the population into the enemy's camp or to the partisans.'

In 1947 the British Military Court held that Kesselring's orders had been an incitement to commit excesses and an instruction to take reprisals. The Field Marshal was held responsible for the actions of the troops under his command.

Field Marshal Kesselring was found guilty on both of the charges and condemned to death by shooting. However, following the representations, the confirming officers commuted the sentence to one of life imprisonment. Among the reasons stated by General Harding for the commutation was that Kesselring's orders were operative for only a limited and relatively short period. However, local massacres of Italian civilians by German troops continued right up to the end of the war.

* * *

Who was Major Barton's target, General 'X?' The most likely German officer was Lieutenant General Max Simon, commander of the 16th SS Panzergrenadier Division *Reichsführer-SS*. The division of 14,683 officers and men had disengaged from general offensive operations to undertake anti-partisan warfare in the Apennines south of Bologna in the summer of 1944. They were to act on Kesselring's directives.

Major Walter Reder, who had lost an arm during the recapture of Kharkov in March 1943, led his armoured reconnaissance group in what became known as the March of Death through Tuscany and Emilia.

During the months of July and August 1944 over 20 punitive actions were carried out against the partisans and the civilian population. More than a thousand Italians were killed, amongst them many women, children and the elderly.

Max Simon relinquished command of the division on 23 October 1944 to lead the 13th SS Panzer Korps. He was replaced by SS-Oberführer Otto Baum on 1 November. The Cisco Red operation began two days later, which explains its failure.

Lieutenant General Simon survived the war unscathed. He was tried by a British military court in Padua in 1947. The commandant was sentenced to death for responsibility in six massacres of Italian civilians. The sentence was also later commuted.

* * *

In January 2007 an Italian Military Court in La Spezia sentenced 10 former members of the 16th SS Division to life imprisonment for their role in the worst World War II massacre of civilians in Western Europe. Compensation of 100 million Euros was also ordered to be paid.

Between 29 September and 5 October 1944, 770 villagers were killed by the SS at Marzabotto, near Bologna, as a reprisal for local Resistance activity. Of the victims, 5 were priests, 316 were females, 250 were minors and 142 were over 60.

The defendants were tried *in absentia*. They are believed to be living in Germany, but, given their ages and the lengthy process of extradition required, none are likely to face prison. In 2005 the court had also sentenced another 10 former SS officers to life imprisonment for the massacre in the Tuscan village of Sant' Anna di Stazzema.

The trials are the outcome of cases reopened after the discovery in 1994 of the so-called 'cupboard of shame.' A locked cabinet in the basement of the Military Prosecutor's office in Rome revealed 694 war crimes files. A third with witness testimonies and requests for action to be taken against suspects had not been acted upon. Enquiries revealed that the documents were shelved in 1960 on political grounds. Italy did not want to prejudice relations with West Germany, an important ally in the Cold War.

NOTES

[1] Narrative based on the Report on Operation Cisco Red by Major BJ Barton, DSO, MC, TNA: PRO HS 6/859.

[2] Charles Macintosh, *From Cloak to Dagger*, p 138.

10 The Old House on the Mountain

On returning to Special Force headquarters in January 1945 after the failure of his mission to kill or capture General 'X,' Major John Barton, DSO, MC, reported that two thousand partisans were active in the plain. However, the rebels were poorly armed and liaison with 5th Army was non-existent. Urgent action was required.

The major suggested that a British mission with a light wireless set could open up the zone. An officer and operator would also be required to establish a base on the fringe of the mountains. They would transmit lengthier messages and maintain contact by courier with the main mission and the partisans.

As a result of this intelligence, a new operation was approved under the leadership of Major Barton with the codename of Cisco Red II. It developed into the Evaporate Mission.

The plan for the penetration of the plain was set out in an order dated 22 January from Lieutenant Colonel Richard Hewitt, new commanding officer of No. 1 Special Force. Captain Neil Oughtred and his signalman, Edward (Ted) Fry, were to form the advance party. They carried a million lire in expenses. The tasks were:

(a) To establish a safe base on the north-eastern slopes of the Apennines.

(b) To organise courier and Intelligence services to the Po Valley and the cities of the plain with a view to the development of resistance in that area.

(c) To pass to base all forms of Intelligence, including bombing targets.

(d) To make all preparations for the reception of the main party under Major Barton who will command the whole mission.

The tasks of the major's group were:

(a) To regain contact with the organisation in the plain either by personal reconnaissance or by the despatch of couriers.

(b) To place the Italian organiser and W/T operator in a safe house in the plain from which contact with base can be established for the passing of tactical messages.

(c) To develop the organisation in the plain for tactical use at the right moment.

(d) To organise dropping grounds in the plain to which stores can be delivered for the use of the clandestine organisation.

Provided the plan was successful, further officers were to be dropped to expand the area. Major Macdermot was briefed and held in readiness to be the first to follow on.

* * *

At dawn on Saturday, 10 February 1945, Captain Oughtred and Signalman Fry parachuted from a Douglas C-47 Dakota onto the northern slopes of the highest peak in the Apennines, Monte Cusna. The field above Case Balocchi, near Asta, in Reggio Emilia was controlled by Captain Michael Lees. Also dropped from the aircraft were two Italian agents of the Goodhue Mission.

Neil Oughtred, aged 26, had joined the Lincolnshire Regiment directly from school. He was tall, courteous and humorous and always had time for people.

Ted Fry related:

Neil was a member of No. 2 Commando. He was wounded during the raid at St Nazaire in France on 28 March 1942. After recovering, the captain rejoined his company in the Mediterranean and took part in commando raids on the Yugoslav islands and mainland. He was then transferred to the Special Operations Executive at Monopoli, near Bari, where we met. We spent a period of training together before flying off on our mission to Reggio Emilia, where we joined the Fioroni family.

Ted Fry had enlisted in the Duke of Cornwall's Regiment in 1942 at age 18. After infantry and tank training he volunteered for airborne operations. Instead there were orders to go for an aptitude test in Morse Code at a manor house near Oxford. Then he was sent to Palestine to undergo signals and parachute instruction. Next stop was Brindisi for intensive coaching in weapons and explosives. Ted Fry related: 'We had an idea what it was all about by then. We were obviously going to be dropped to do a wireless job.'

Ted Fry recalled the parachute landing at Case Balocchi:

Being young and fit, the thought of the flight into the unknown conveyed no anxiety at all. As I had no knowledge of the situation

108

in the area of Villa Minozzo, I could not know what to expect. Captain Oughtred on the other hand, having seen active service with the Commandos and being wounded in coastal raids to France, did feel a bit apprehensive. I recall him saying that if the rum he took a good swig at was too much, would I kick him out. This was not necessary and we parted company with the aircraft. Through the scattered cloud we could see the mountain peaks below. Not a very good landing, but fortunately my canopy got caught in a tall tree. I swung through a gap between the tree and the burnt timbers of a house into the soft snow. I thought I was going into the house itself, which could have been nasty.

We were met by a truly fascinating, elderly rascal with a beautiful white beard under the *nome di battaglia* of Scalabrino who will forever be etched in my memory, if only for the great helping of Lambrusco which he pressed me to drink. He handed us over to 'Noris,' a striking partisan girl with the strength of a lion, assigned to lead us down the treacherous, icy tracks to Secchio, a small mountain village where the British Envelope Mission was established.

We found the liaison officer, Captain Mike Lees, his aide, Lieutenant Smith, and Wireless Operator, Bert Farrimond, ensconced in the house of the priest, Don Pietro Rivi. They had arrived a few weeks earlier and had taken over the mission from Major Vivian Johnston. I believe he was the first to arrive in the Apennines (on 12 June 1944) to link up with the resistance groups for the purpose of receiving further missions. The twenty-seventh of July saw the arrival of Major Jim Davies, Ernest Wilcockson, Charles Holland, and their group for the Montefiorino area, but alas they were soon to pull away due to the great enemy activity, and moved west where they continued to operate.

We moved on to a house on a knoll [the Fioroni dwelling on Monte Costabona], with a panoramic view of the whole area, a house which I believe saw more movement and action than any other in the north of Italy. From here signals were viewed for many miles and gave warnings or otherwise of the state of enemy movements even over into the province of Modena. It was here that we parted with our two Italian colleagues who moved down towards the plains, but regrettably I understand these brave lads were captured and of course executed.

We were to form our base here at Costabona with which to set up staging posts down to the plain for a Major Barton (or Stone as he was known) to operate. Whether the loss of the two Italian agents altered these arrangements I am not sure. I gather Major Barton and his Wireless Operator, Charlie Barratt, took a blind drop on 20-21 March with Mission Evaporate.

At the *Casa Vecchia* [the old house], as it is has been called, we were met by a true Italian mother, Signora Maria Bertolini Fioroni, a lady of tiny stature but with a heart of gold and the courage that can only be found in a chosen few. She introduced us to 'Don Carlo,' Don Domenico Orlandini, leader of the partisan group the *Fiamme Verdi*, a devoted member of the Resistance. Not enough has been written of his exploits in aiding Allied prisoners of war to escape from captivity. Until the time of his untimely death in 1977 he remained a true friend to me on my return visits to this lovely land. I sadly miss the tap on the shoulder at Villa Minozzo market place and the friendly greeting *'Ciao, Ted,'* from this legendary, brave and so gentle man.

Captain Oughtred and I spent our first night 'with the priest,' a local phrase describing a wonderfully simple bed warmer made of a wooden frame which contained a small pot of glowing charcoal, sheer bliss amidst the snow and ice. Mamma Maria, as I have since been honoured to call her, made up an English breakfast of fried bacon and eggs. She introduced us to her sons: Domenico and Romolo who were in the *Fiamme Verdi,* and the younger three, Tito, Romano and Cesare, who whilst only boys still helped out with the mules and relayed messages. [1]

Signora Fioroni was the schoolteacher in the Costabona elementary school from 1923 to 1958. She had been widowed at age 41 in 1941 when her husband, Prospero, an Italian Army infantry captain, was killed on the Greek-Albanian border.

After the war, Signora Fioroni recalled:

During the Resistance the life in our mountain villages was always hard and difficult. To the shortage of men required to carry out daily work of all kinds must be added the need to assist those who had taken up arms. Costabona, owing to its geographical and strategic position at the centre of the Reggio partisan zone, and its direct contact with that of Modena, was for a long time simultaneously the seat of the partisan command, several detachments, and the Allied missions.

All the protagonists of the War of Liberation, of every race and nationality, passed through our house on the mountain, and they found every form of assistance. The thought of my sons under arms and far away, and our innate and strong sense of hospitality, led me to do unprecedented things in favour of those in need. For us the nicest form of recognition comes in the British officers and soldiers who return to visit almost every year.

If the life was therefore difficult in moments of calm, it became impossible in the course of the constant roundups by the Germans and Fascists. The one in January 1945, in particular, was terrible.

Romolo Fioroni, the partisan *Franco,* recalled the British mission:

To my mother, Captain Oughtred and his telegraphist, Ted, were not merely guests or persons in difficulty to help and protect. Very soon they became sons, treated the same as the other five. And her home was their home...

Many foreigners and Italians in addition to Captain Oughtred's mission found hospitality in the old house on the mountain on a long-term or occasional basis. So much so that when we boys returned on leave from partisan operations we had to sleep in the barn. Because this is what Mamma Maria insisted upon. Hospitality came first.

Strategy meetings were often held. They took place in the ancient, vast kitchen, around the hearth in which a large fire burnt day and night. The heads of the British missions, captains Lees and Oughtred, were to be found there together with Commandant 'Monti,' 'Carlo,' 'Barbanera' and many others. After dinner there was always the gathering around the fire, the regulation glass of *grappa* and the long discussions. [2]

Ted Fry added:

Mamma Maria, Anita in the kitchen, and of course the elderly grandmother, Dina, and an aunt to the five boys, were fully occupied in feeding the huge gatherings of visitors to the old house with whatever food could be found in these difficult times.

Polenta was in great demand because of the many different factions. The Resistance groups were mainly local, but of course a large number of people arrived for help or to escape transportation, coming from as far as Sicily!

I recall the small family groups that periodically arrived for sustenance, on their way from the coast at Massa carrying packs of salt on their backs, braving the snow and ice through the mountain passes in order to help them exist in the World which had been so cruel to so many millions. [3]

This is Captain Oughtred's report on the mission. Throughout he refers to Major Barton under his pseudonym of Stone.

My job was to establish a secure mountain base on the northern slopes of the Apennines. This HQ was to act as a supply and communications post for Major Stone who was to operate in the plain. I was also to create a courier system from my mission to the main cities of the plain in order to facilitate the sending of messages between the major and myself.

I established my mission at Costabona and spent the first week with Captain Lees, learning the local situation, contacting partisan leaders, and recruiting couriers and personnel for defence. I was also in touch with Major Davies of Silentia Mission and with an OSS team in the Modena province.

Efforts were made to contact the Resistance leaders in the cities of Reggio and Modena provinces and to arrange the courier system. Contact was made with HQ SAP [*Squadre d' Azione Partigiana*, or Squads of Partisan Action] and GAP [*Gruppi d' Azione Patriottica*, or Groups of Patriotic Action] Reggio and a courier system was established. It ran from mission HQ to a checkpoint at Viano and from there to the cities and towns of Reggio province.

Contact was also made with the partisans of Modena, but they were very suspicious and not inclined to cooperate. However, they finally agreed to accept and deliver messages, both from the mission and from Major Stone on his arrival. Further efforts were made and a good contact was established with HQ Carpi and also with the surrounding towns. A satisfactory system was established quite independently of the one to Modena.

Some difficulty was encountered in that the interest of the partisans tended to decrease when they found that we were not going to supply them with large quantities of arms and ammunition.

Several reconnaissances were also made with a view to moving the mission nearer to the plain, thus cutting down the time spent by the couriers on the road. To this end a number of bicycles were also purchased.

The finding of a suitable location for the mission presented some difficulty in that the organised partisan area in the Reggio Province extended only as far as the River Secchia, which was itself some eight hours march from the edge of the plain.

Beyond the river there was only a very loose and undisciplined organisation of mountain SAP who were completely without adequate arms and therefore could offer very little resistance in the case of an enemy drive.

There were also many roads in the area suitable for motorised transport. Routes shown on the map as being usable only by mules were often good enough to take a 15-cwt lorry. The Germans both could and did use these roads and on occasion were able to arrive with very little warning.

It was suggested that the mission might take control of this partisan formation and arm and organise them. But Captain Lees, under whose influence they came, was very much against the idea and it was temporarily abandoned.

Finally, an agreement was made with the local SAP leader, 'Bortaise,' for a system whereby immediate warning was to be given to the mission in the event of the approach of the enemy. It was decided to establish the HQ at Monte Largo in the Vallestra area as soon as it was certain when Major Stone was likely to be arriving.

The position occupied by the SAP organisation under 'Bortaise' was somewhat difficult as they came between two definite organisations, the mountain partisans south of the River Secchia and the SAP and GAP organisations of the plain, which began in the Viano area. From neither of these organisations did they receive regular supplies, so that they had to beg arms and munitions when and where they could.

'Bortaise' himself previously commanded the SAP in the Reggio area but retired to the mountains owing to ill health. He was nominally Communist but seemed to have very few political views. The strength of his band was about two hundred, but these were very poorly armed and morale was low as they felt that they were being neglected and mistrusted. They saw the partisans living on the south side of the Secchia receiving arms and supplies, whilst they on the north bank and in closer contact with the enemy had the greatest difficulty in obtaining necessities of any sort.

Owing to their low morale, the partisans' discipline was bad and it was only with great difficulty that they could be persuaded to stand and fight. They had to a certain extent lost faith in the British as they had in the past been promised arms and supplies and then later been refused.

Partisan reaction to Allied propaganda was good, but I consider that the 'go slow' directive was unnecessary as I have generally found that the partisans require no encouragement to follow this policy.

On 6 March a message was received from Major Stone stating that he would be dropping in the Carpi area after the 12th. HQ Carpi were immediately warned and they agreed to keep a strict watch for his arrival.

On 12 March the mission moved forward as arranged to Monte Largo in the Vallestra area. We remained for 36 hours before having to withdraw to Cavola owing to the arrival of a strong enemy patrol in the immediate neighbourhood. They were reliably reported to be looking for us. The Germans eventually came within five hundred yards of our HQ, but this was some time after we had left.

The mission remained at Cavola for three days and was then forced to withdraw again owing to an enemy drive across the River Secchia at Cerredolo, which threatened to spread along the river. We retreated to Percola di Cavola and established a rear base of stores and food. Two days later a small party, consisting of W/T operator, three partisan guards and myself, returned to the Vallestra area by night. We established a HQ at San Apollinare and were able to remain for eight days.

During this period we were somewhat troubled by spies and two of them were caught by the local SAP.

Constant efforts were made to contact Major Stone whose arrival had been postponed on several occasions. When on 22 March a message was received from base stating that he had definitely dropped on the previous night, these attempts were intensified but without success. Nor was any news heard of him. It was presumed that the major had gone to ground. HQ Carpi stated that he had not arrived in their area. Enquiries were made in other zones but without result.

During this period it was decided to give a limited amount of arms to the SAP under 'Bortaise' and a target zone was chosen in the Vallestra area. On 22 March a drop was received. Unfortunately, it was only possible to receive one plane owing to the enemy occupation of Carpineti and to the complete inability of the SAP to put up any resistance to a push from this direction. However, all stores were safely delivered, collected and distributed. The morale of the partisans, which had been at rather a low ebb, improved considerably, as did their efforts to assist us in every way.

On the night of 23 March the enemy started a drive up the Viano-Baiso-Vallestra road. In spite of some resistance by both Fifth Zone of the SAP on the plain and the mountain SAP under 'Bortaise,' by the 26th the Germans had occupied Viano, Baiso, Gatta, Levizzano and Castello di Carpineti. They now controlled the main partisan link with the plain, and from Castello di Carpineti completely overlooked the whole of the Vallestra area.

There were also rumours of a full-scale roundup in the zones of Carpi, Mirandola and Rubiera. Partisans from all these areas passed through our territory. Men from one of the Carpi brigades had heard that Major Stone was operating somewhere to the north of the town.

On the night of 26 March the SAP crossed the River Secchia into partisan territory and the mission followed next day owing to the presence of enemy patrols in the Vallestra area which threatened to cut us off. We withdrew to our base at Percola di Cavola.

The next two days were spent reorganising the SAP and sending patrols across the river, both of partisans and of mission personnel. On 30 March the enemy withdrew from Baiso, Levizzano and Castello di Carpineti, but left a strong garrison at Gatta and also a number of troops at Carpineti and in the immediate area. The SAP sent over further patrols and on 31 March the main body recrossed the Secchia with the intention of occupying Vallestra and then pushing down towards Baiso. It was arranged for the mission to follow on 1 April.

However, on the night of 31 March an enemy force of between three and four hundred men crossed the river at Gatta and Ponte di Cavola and pushed towards Quara. A strong patrol came to the house occupied by the mission at Percola di Cavola, but fortunately we had received warning and were able to withdraw after some firing.

The mission proceeded to Quara. After disposing of the wireless set, we took part in the subsequent counter-attack. After the enemy had withdrawn across the river the mission moved to Cerré Marabino and re-established contact with 'Bortaise' and his SAP and agreed to give them further arms. The formation was to remain under the direct control of the mission.

On 9 April a message was received from base ordering me to close down the operation, hand the set over to Envelope Mission and to proceed to Parma Province and join Major Holland. I arrived at his HQ on 14 April, having taken four days to reach him owing to a minor roundup in Reggio province, which made it necessary for me to go north to La Vecchia before crossing Route 63.

For the time being, Ted Fry remained in the mountains. Neil Oughtred concluded his report with:

Local conditions were good. There was no apparent food shortage except of luxuries such as coffee and sugar. There was, however, a fairly general lack of salt and of fats.

The attitude of the civilians was friendly, but nearer the plain they did not encourage a long stay and although quite willing to produce food preferred that not more than one night be spent in any house.

All stores dropped were useful and in most cases arrived in good condition.

W/T: Communications were one hundred per cent satisfactory. [4]

The partisan leader mentioned in the report under the pseudonym of Bortaise was Gismondo Veroni. He joined the underground Communist party in 1931, served in the army for eight years and was one of the first leaders of armed resistance in Reggio Emilia following the September 1943 Armistice.

Gismondo Veroni became commandant of the provincial SAP and, as mentioned in the Special Force report, later led the mountain formation, which was the *285th Brigata SAP*. He was awarded the Italian Silver Medal for Military Valour.

During the final offensive, SOE personnel formed forward parties to liase between the partisans and the advancing Fifth Army. Neil Oughtred witnessed the liberation of Parma and Ted Fry that of Reggio Emilia. The captain became deputy governor of the Asti province of Piedmont under the Allied Military Government (AMG). After a period of leave in England, Ted Fry sailed to India to join another SOE operation, Force 136. He was Mentioned in Despatches.

After the war, the two friends frequently took the mule track up to 'the old house on the mountain' at Costabona to revisit their 'Italian mother' and the rest of the Fioroni family.

NOTES

[1] Eddy Fry, 'The British Mission to the Apennines above Reggio,' *No. 1 Special Force and Italian Resistance*, pp 256-7.
[2] Romolo Fioroni, 'Neil Oughtred,' *Reggiostoria*, No. 103, April - June 2004. The translations of this and other Italian sources are mine.
[3] Fry, op. cit., p 259. Anita was an elderly lady of Slavic origin who helped in the running of the house. The aunt was Dina's sister, Maria.
[4] Report on the Activities of the Cisco Mission, TNA: PRO HS 6/863.

Ted Fry in Siena for debriefing after the mission, 1945.

The former SOE men with the Fioroni family at Costabona in 1987. Neil Oughtred is at the head of the table and Ted Fry on the right.

Ted Fry with the ox cart in which the group moved down from the mountains at the end of the war, 2005.

11 The Plains Partisans

The main party of the Special Force Cisco Red II mission to support partisans on the plain left in March 1945. It was led by Major John Barton, DSO, MC, an experienced agent, as we saw in Chapter 9.

The rebels were unable to provide a drop zone or reception party owing to the open terrain and number of enemy soldiers in the area.

Major Barton volunteered to jump to the most inaccessible place Captain Oughtred could find for him. The plan had to be cancelled at the last minute because the major needed urgent medical treatment. Two days later, the parachute drop was able to go ahead.

The group consisted of Major Barton; the wireless operator, Sergeant Charles Barratt, who had returned from the Silentia Mission with Major Wilcockson; and two Italian brothers, Gino and Mario Barbera. Kit was kept to a minimum and the drop slated for the early hours. From experience the major knew that the quietest time on the plain was between midnight and 2am.

John Barton recalled:

> We took off from Rosignano Airport in a Liberator on 20 March at 23.00 hours with the intention of blind dropping into a DZ midway between Carpi and the River Secchia. I was disappointed that the American crew were inexperienced at this type of work, also that we had no dispatcher, only the rear-gunner who was unsure of himself. I was able to talk to the crew before we left and gave them a picture of the ground situation and also impressed on them the necessity of getting rid of the packages with the personnel so that they would drop near us and we could find them in the dark.
>
> In bright moonlight, we arrived over the target area about 00.30 hours. After several circuits and a message from the navigator that he wasn't sure if this was the DZ or not, we jumped in the order: myself, Barratt, Mario and Gino.
>
> It was a good drop and we saw no signs of transport or movement on the roads. As arranged beforehand, Gino, the last man out, flicked his torch and we joined him and started looking for the two packages. We found one with a B2 set in it only 30 yards away. We spent nearly an hour looking for the other container. As there was no sign of it, we decided to wait until first light.

We packed our parachutes, hid them under some bushes and moved in an easterly direction until we struck the River Secchia. I had no idea of our location, so we went to a farmhouse and found out that we were about 4 miles north of Bondanello and some 30 kilometres north of our DZ. A few more seconds flying time would have seen us north of the Po instead of south.

We made the farmer guide us to the village. After a lot of trouble we found a man who was vaguely connected with the partisans in Concordia and who promised to get in touch with them and send a patrol to fetch us the following night. The bridge at Bondanello was unguarded and quite a lot of transport was moving over it, going north to the Po. There was no difficulty crossing.

I knew nothing about this area at all except that there were no partisans and that it was considered a very bad Fascist zone. So we were lucky to call on non-Fascist houses.

We moved back to the dropping ground under cover of an early morning mist, buried our parachutes and jump suits and made a thorough search for the missing container. When it was too light to look any more we hid in a hayloft and had a few hours sleep. About 11 o'clock a girl ran in to tell us that the container had been found a mile away by the Fascists, that a farmer had seen us drop and that they were searching the area.

This was bad, and being inside a hayloft with only revolvers even worse, so we made the farmer conceal us under some straw in his cart and take us into the countryside. Here we hid in a ditch and watched the search. It was by no means thorough and the Fascists went away at dusk.

The promised partisan patrol failed to turn up, so at midnight we went to Bondanello and found a guide to the Concordia partisans.

A lot of heavy-duty vehicles and ammunition trucks were crossing the bridge. I noticed a dump of American butterfly bombs, which I was told had been dropped recently. The Hun had been very scared of them and there had been several casualties. Section positions and gun sites had been dug all along the banks of the Secchia by the *Todt* [forced labour] organisation.

We walked about 10 kilometres and stopped in a small village north of Concordia. We were hidden by a farmer in a little hole built under the stable. The Germans were digging an 88mm gun position in his garden.

The next night, the local partisan chief came and accused us of being spies and made things very difficult. However, we were finally accepted and went away with him to a very good hideout in the middle of a ploughed field. We spent 10 days in this hole with a section of partisans. At dusk a local farmer would come and dig open the entrance for us, and at dawn he dug us in. On the second day, a German patrol came and took him away for questioning, but fortunately didn't notice what he was doing.

This was the beginning of a roundup which had as its object the terrorising of partisans and civilians in order to safeguard a large movement of troops to the north of the Po. Nobody was allowed in or near the main northern routes, everybody was rounded up for questioning and the younger men taken away for the *Todt*. The troops concerned in the move turned out to be the 29th Panzer Grenadier Division and I was fortunate enough to be able to follow all its movements from the time the vanguard crossed the Concordia bridge until the general and his staff left their house outside Mirandola en route for Bondeno and later Comachio. The Air Force made a successful night attack on this division.

During my 10-day stay with the Concordia battalion the future looked very dismal. They were unarmed, dispirited, afraid and in the process of disbanding and going to the mountains. Their organisation had fallen to pieces under determined German and Fascist roundups and they had no good leaders. They were not inclined to cooperate and were controlled by the Communist elements amongst them.

I found it quite impossible to make wireless contact during the night and had to send Barratt away by himself to transmit from a different house each day, but after a few times the civilians refused to have him in their houses because they were too afraid.

Although I felt sure the outlook was not as bad at Carpi or Mirandola, it was obvious that the original intention of using a mountain base was not feasible and that the time factor given me by both 5th and 8th armies before I was dropped prevented any further infiltration. Accordingly, I signalled Major Macdermot to stand down and that Captain Oughtred at mountain base should be used by some other mission. It was disappointing, but there was no alternative.

The Concordia commandant was called Gianni and his real name was Cesare Buganza. He was a 20-year-old Communist. I put Mario Barbera with him and that produced very good results. The partisans stopped leaving for the mountains, reformed and reorganised and after a while made a very good intelligence service. Their enthusiasm as I had known it over Christmas returned and they cooperated as best they could.

All movements over Concordia, Bondanello and Quistello bridges were reported and enemy formations in the area known. It was difficult, however, as the Germans didn't give anything away and anybody showing curiosity was immediately taken away to Modena. The Fascists were far crueller and more ruthless than the Germans and torturing a partisan before shooting him was quite normal. Women spies were used a great deal on both sides.

After the liberation we found that the Fascist Gestapo had a man out after us and that the Germans had two detection vans trying to locate our radio. Our move into the Mirandola area probably saved us.

The German soldiers were guarded in their conversations with civilians, although they would admit that they had lost the war and were tired of it all.

The fighter-bombers did some excellent work by day and the medium bombers visited the Po crossings nightly, yet the accuracy of the bombing was poor and civilians and their homes suffered more than the Germans.

Mario remained with his battalion until he was overrun, and kept me informed by courier. The results achieved by his men between 20-23 April are proof of the good work he did.

I sent daily messages to Carpi to ask the formation there to come and fetch us, but at first the messages were captured, and then they refused to believe we were not spies. After 10 days I had still made no contact. I knew there was an OSS mission somewhere near Carpi, so I decided to leave the brigade in their hands and see what I could do in the Mirandola area. On 1 April I made contact with the Remo Brigade and the following night left for their HQ.

From this time until we were overrun there was only one thing beating us. That was the time factor. There was so much to do. As soon as the partisans realised we were going to support them with arms, ammunition and money, they regained all their old enthusiasm. There was not the freedom of movement and contempt for the Germans that there had been before, but the brigade improved daily and quickly organised an intelligence system. Information came direct to me from every battalion. When the arms arrived, a German was killed almost nightly and sabotage broke out all over the area.

The Remo Brigade received its orders from Modena and was one of the formations in the 2nd Modena Division. It was about 800 strong, with hundreds of supporters ready to help when it was certain the Allies would come. About half the strength of the brigade lived in holes underground, while the other half lived quite openly amongst the Germans and in many cases were employed by them. There were five battalions forming the brigade.

Major Barton described the leading personalities, including the Commandant:

Giuseppe Ferraresi alias Polo, brigade commander and captain in the regular army. A very intelligent, fine personality with a natural command of his men. He was captured at Cremona on 9 September 1943 by SS troops but escaped to his family at Mirandola. He joined the partisans in March 1944, became commandant and in February 1945 took over the Remo Brigade. I have the highest admiration for this man and consider him the finest partisan I have met. He lived amongst the Germans quite openly, yet controlled his brigade in a very efficient manner and gave me all possible cooperation. Brave and completely honest, he is now working for the CLN in Modena.

The other officers of the brigade were the commissar, Tullio Paltrineri alias Ivo, a Communist, and two former Italian Air Force pilots, Giuseppe Saraceno known as Libero, the chief of staff, and Renzo Fornasari alias Dionisio, the intelligence officer, both independents.

Major Barton continued:

I was able to move about the area comparatively easily at night. There were only two or three bicycle rides as the roads were too well patrolled and had numerous roadblocks. Movement along the adjoining fields, however, presented no difficulty. I stayed with each of the battalion commanders and arranged for the arming and organising of their men. When the question of the dropping of arms was first discussed it was turned down as impossible, but after a while the partisans became very interested and gave me their whole support.

Two dropping grounds were chosen in order to facilitate the distribution of arms, one on a flat open piece of ground between two secondary roads and the other in the centre of a large wood. This proved superior, as if a container was not found it would not be noticed during the daytime and could be looked for on the following night.

We depended entirely on the BBC messages to warn all concerned about a drop and it worked well. We used ordinary torches for recognition signals, although with Eureka [the ground-based radar homing device working to a set in an aircraft] no lights were necessary.

The first few drops were very poor. The planes came in too high and one spread its load over a distance of two miles. The Germans found most of the containers in the morning. Another aircraft dropped a complete load 12 miles away from the DZ in the middle of Route 12.

The best drop of all was pure luck. There must have been a mistake in the timing because an hour before the mission was due I heard a plane fly in rather low. For no reason at all I flashed the signal letter, which was K, in its direction. The pilot made a half circuit and dropped his complete cargo all around me - no lights, no Eureka and no partisans to take the containers away.

On the night of 19 April we received three planes between 23.00 and 23.30 hours - and at midnight the Germans were using the ground.

The collecting and hiding of the containers and the distribution of the contents, I left entirely to the partisans. Never once did they let me down. The distribution was made fairly and everybody finally had a weapon and some ammunition. Gino used to go round to the various battalions and explain the operation of the Bren guns. He made a very good job of this and worked hard.

In 12 days the brigade received 10 Liberator loads of arms and ammunition. The Eureka was a great asset to us and worked perfectly. I cannot say why the Germans did not stop these drops or ambush us on the dropping ground.

The enemy definitely knew they were going on because they found quite a few of the containers and everybody was aware that the partisans were being armed by a British mission. There were quite a few troops all around us and, although they might not have caught us, they could easily have taken action to prevent the drops. By changing our recognition signal nightly there was little chance of the planes being deceived by a decoy, yet as far as I am aware even this was not attempted by the enemy.

On 14 April we ran into a little trouble. At about 15.00 hours we were in a house which was thought to be fairly safe. Barratt was transmitting upstairs while I was sitting downstairs talking to some partisans. A patrol of *Brigata Nera* [the Black Brigade] surrounded the house without our knowing. An officer walked in and asked for my papers. He was killed, but not before he had warned the others.

As we were virtually unarmed things looked bad, but by good fortune there was a section of partisans living in a hole in a nearby house. They had received their Bren and Sten guns only the previous night and came out firing everything they had, completely routing the *Brigata Nera.*

The Fascists ran away and returned with reinforcements, but by this time the whole partisan battalion had turned out with their new weapons and quite a battle developed. The partisans again chased the militia away, killing five of their officers and a German Regimental Sergeant Major (RSM), with no casualties to themselves.

The German garrison heard the firing and took it to be an Allied airborne landing, not believing that there were any partisans at all in that particular area. The number of rounds fired would certainly have done credit to a British division putting in an attack.

The Fascists later returned and burned down the house and shot the owner. They mutilated the body of the officer killed there and took it to Mirandola as a proof of partisan atrocity. The heartening part of this affair, however, was the partisans' willingness to fight and the stimulating effect it had on their morale.

On 20 April I received the order for an all-out partisan effort. They were dubious at first because the enemy did not appear to be pulling out of our area at all, but towards evening the rush to the Po commenced and everybody started coming out in the open and firing on the retreating columns.

There was considerable confusion on account of Italian paratroops being dropped [on the Allied side], without any password to identify themselves or any coordinated effort being made with the partisans. The paratroops did good work, but there would have been four times as much accomplished if only there had been some liaison and coordination.

It was a big disappointment, both to the partisans and myself, that we were not required in the Herring Operation [to sabotage and disrupt the enemy retreat].

For the first two days the brigade confined itself to harassing operations, but on the 22nd formations took over towns and villages and handed them over some hours later. Among the places were Cavezzo, Medolla, San Possidonio, Concordia and finally Mirandola.

An American armoured column passed my HQ, which was five miles south of Mirandola, at 15.00 hours. So we put the set in a donkey cart and trotted along Route 12 into the town. The Americans had turned west just after passing us and we found quite a lot of German transport and troops. But in the dusk they mistook us for Fascists, with our black berets, and did not stop the cart.

I found two partisan battalions already in Mirandola and by 23.00 hours another had arrived and the town was completely cleared of all enemy troops, roadblocks established, partisans patrolling the streets and the CLN having its first official meeting.

At 01.00 hours the Americans started to shell and mortar the town. After three hours of this wanton destruction, I took Barratt, the brigade commander and a partisan out of the town to try and locate the gunfire and stop it.

We went south in the direction of S. Felice. It was too slow walking so I borrowed a bicycle and went on ahead with the partisan. About a mile along the road we came to a crossroads with a barrier. Seeing a couple of men in the shade of a wall I shouted out to them. Somebody answered 'Hell,' so I immediately took them to be Americans and cycled over to shake hands. I realised too late that they were Germans.

Although I tried to convince them that I was a Fascist, one of the soldiers was suspicious and insisted I come with him into their guardroom. They treated me politely, took away my binoculars and marched me off to an officer. He was in bed and refused to see me until morning. I was put with the partisan and a guard in a room with a few chairs in it. Here I spent the night, disposing of signal plans and several other compromising documents. In the morning I saw a German captain, but he did not interrogate me and mistook me for a forward patrol of the 5th Army, which was fortunate.

There was about a platoon of the enemy. Their discipline was good when an officer or the RSM were about, but when I started talking to them I found they were infantry doing demolition and rearguard and were tired of fighting and wanted it to finish quickly. They were too frightened of the captain to desert or let me escape, although one corporal promised he would flee with me later on when he thought it would be safer. About midday, American infantry put in an attack and I escaped with the partisan. Most of my captors surrendered.

During the last three days the partisans killed or took prisoner over a thousand Germans and Fascists, prevented the destruction of the bridges at Concordia and Bondanello and destroyed 30 trucks, 4 tanks, 32 horse carts and 2 medium calibre artillery. The bridge at Pioppa was successfully blown by the partisans on 20 April. They behaved extraordinarily well and after the initial enthusiasm had passed, remained calm and orderly.

Every town and village had its CLN elected and ready to take over when the Germans left. This they did with an efficiency that surprised me. Towns were cleared of debris, anti-tank obstacles filled in and public services repaired where necessary. Life returned to normal under their supervision in a very short time.

CIC [Counter-Intelligence Corps] arrived on the heels of the forward troops and I did what I could to help them, but they did not stay long enough. After these came an Allied Military Government (AMG) official and he spoke to the CLNs and told them what he wanted done. Before he left, he ordered the partisans to release their Fascist prisoners and allow them to remain in their homes until they could be tried. This order quite naturally resulted in riots, lynching mobs and demonstrations.

The whole attitude towards the Fascists was pathetic. Here were men who had tortured and killed the families and relations of these people and there was no certainty that they would receive justice.

Some of the Fascists were taken away to Modena and within a week were seen marching in the partisan disarmament parade there.

As a result of this lack of vision by AMG, a wave of murder spread through the area and it was extremely difficult to check it.

No other AMG official came near for a week or more and so the partisans took over full control, policing and reorganising the area. On 12 May the brigade disarmed except for a small police force. There were no incidents or clashes with Allied troops except a few Negro soldiers who terrorised some of the women. The American police force arrived and dealt with these types.

I have recently been back to the area to liquidate certain claims. In Concordia the Communist party is behaving nearly as badly as the Fascists and the people are unhappy, but elsewhere all is well and the CLNs are doing good work.

It is hard to say whether the mission could have operated and received drops before it did. The Germans were hard pushed when we arrived and the enemy offensive gave them no spare troops to clean up the partisan movement along their lines of communication.

I think we were fortunate to get away with so many drops and comparatively few casualties. Sergeant Barratt and the Barbera brothers were first class and I was lucky to have them.

Barratt remained calm and cheerful under the most difficult circumstances and was a tremendous help. At all times his one thought was to pass all the messages I gave him and he never failed in this. He was brave and resourceful at all times.

I consider the partisans on the plain deserved all the support we gave them and fully justified themselves as brave patriots. [1]

After the war, former Special Force members recalled their encounters with John Barton. Major Charles Macintosh, described him as 'a remarkable young man.' Major Ernest Wilcockson said that he was 'a mystery man with a secret mission who was never a proper member of SOE.' Major Jim Davies related that he was 'a splendid fellow from Monopoli or Siena, I think, from another "funny" service.'

* * *

The facts were often stranger than fiction in wartime. This is also evident in the next chapter. The partisan leader was the village priest.

NOTES

[1] Narrative based on The Report on Evaporate Mission by Major BJ Barton, DSO, MC, TNA: PRO HS 6/859.

12 SAS and the Green Flames

On 21 March 1945 Fascists in the Province of Reggio Emilia in western Emilia wrote about the local rebel priest:

> Carlo Orlandini from the hamlet of Poiano in Villa Minozzo is actually commandant of the bandit formation known as the Green Flames ... he has participated in many attacks on Republican Guard garrisons across the mountains. Orlandini has led partisan groups against Italian and German troops during roundups and is always distinctive for his harsh and cruel spirit.

In the high country of Reggio Emilia armed resistance was led by 'white partisans.' These were Roman Catholics and democrats who were explicitly not 'red partisans.' For patriotic reasons they called themselves the Green Flames. The name was inspired by the distinctive collar patch of the elite mountain corps of the Italian Army, the *Alpini.* The commandant of the partisan formation was Don Domenico Orlandini, known as Don Carlo.

At the end of the war, the Green Flames wrote in their periodical *'La Penna,'*:

> Perhaps someone who sees him today for the first time would not be able to credit that this young man - so thin, with his friendly little smile, and at times a little ironic - would have been able to carry out such energetic deeds.
>
> But we who lived with him know that there were moments in which even his strength as a man would have been sorely tried if he had not been sustained by his patriotic faith, his religious fervour and his mountain steadfastness.
>
> We know that when he was in our midst in periods of calm, in the few of those he had, he was a man, like any other man. But when the hour for action approached he was everywhere, on horseback and on foot, and his smile inspired trust and serenity. Then he left for the attack at the head of his partisans.

The province provided a refuge to many Allied escaped prisoners of war and disbanded Italian soldiers. The fugitives were concentrated in the mountains of the Secchia Valley, a landscape of green pastures and deciduous woods beneath the highest peaks of the Tuscan-Emilian Apennines.

In September 1943 Don Orlandini was the priest at Poiano, a hamlet in the large commune of Villa Minozzo in the south of the province, which also accommodated the old house on the mountain at Costabona. He was a member of an anti-Fascist organisation based in the provincial capital, Reggio Emilia. On the 15th Don Orlandini became commandant of a newly formed Mountain Battalion of partisans. He also helped create a support network for Allied prisoners of war. They were directed along an escape line that ran across the Apennine ridge to the east coast and linked up with Allied rescue craft.

On 4 October Don Orlandini disappeared from the mountains. Apart from a brief visit in November, he was not seen again until April 1944. Main responsibility for the welfare of the fugitives passed to his friend, 40-year-old Don Pasquino Borghi, the new priest in the hamlet of Tapignola, five kilometres above Villa Minozzo. He spoke English fluently after having served as a missionary for seven years in the Anglo-Egyptian Sudan.

Don Borghi was a fervent democrat and openly voiced his criticism of the Fascists. He placed himself at the disposal of the provincial liberation committee and adopted the *nome di battaglia* of Albertario. The priest provided food, clothing and accommodation for Allied escaped prisoners of war, youngsters avoiding the call up, and partisans. After the war, Don Orlandini related that about 50 former prisoners had received sanctuary in the rectory at Tapignola.

Parishioners thought that Don Borghi was too trusting and perhaps a little innocent. Fellow clerics and members of the Resistance urged him to be more prudent. Some of the fugitives were sent to houses owned by the church in Cervarolo, but Don Borghi refused to stop harbouring partisans. He said: 'Where can I send these poor lads if no one else wants to shelter them?'

Among the fighters were eight members of the Cervi band from Gattatico on the plain. Their leaders, seven brothers, had been executed by the Fascists on 28 December 1943. The survivors launched a robbery on the post office at Cinquecerri on 17 January 1944. Fascist militia intervened and one was killed, the first loss they had sustained.

Four days later, Don Borghi walked down to Villa Minozzo to celebrate the feast of Saint Agnes with girls of the Catholic Action movement. He exchanged greetings with a patrol of *Carabinieri* and Fascist militia that he met on the way, little realising that they were bound for his rectory.

The troops found that a schoolmistress was teaching young children on the ground floor of the building. Everything seemed normal. However, when the search moved upstairs the men were met by rifle fire as they disturbed a number of partisans in hiding. No one was hurt, but the outnumbered Fascists retreated.

By evening, Don Borghi was tracked down in Villa Minozzo and soon arrested. He was imprisoned in the gaol at Servi and then transferred to Scandiano prison.

A week later, the first National Guard commander was killed by other partisans in the Correggio area. Immediate reprisals were ordered. The political prisoners were to be treated as simple hostages. On 29 January Don Borghi and eight partisans were condemned to death. They were shot on the firing range at Reggio Emilia the following morning.

Don Pasquino Borghi was posthumously awarded the Italian *Medaglia d'Oro al Valor Militare*, the Gold Medal for Military Valour.

Don Domenico Orlandini returned to the mountains in April. He was wearing British uniform and had adopted the *nome di battaglia* of Carlo. From then on he was known affectionately to his men as Don Carlo.

Only after the war was he able to tell his full story:

The sight of the Allied prisoners of war - hungry, covered in rags, fearful of again falling into the hands of the Germans or Fascists, and unsure who to trust - led me to take a decision that I was already toying with: to cross the lines.

This would enable me to make the contacts I considered vital to organising the resistance in the mountains on a much wider scale. At the same time I would be able to agree a plan with the Allies for the rescue of the endangered prisoners scattered across our mountains and in other areas of the Apennines.

The lawyer Pellizzi and my other friends in Reggio fully approved of my plan. At the time I had two South African majors in my house at Poiano. I also discussed the project with them and they gave me a letter of introduction and recommendation for the Allied commanders.

The priest became an agent of A Force, the Allied deception and escape agency, which was part of military intelligence. On the night of 3 November he was a member of a sabotage squad that disembarked from a motorboat near Ancona. Rome Radio falsely claimed that the raiders had been captured. One was said to have been dressed as a priest.

At the end of the mission, Don Orlandini returned to the Secchia Valley for three weeks. He brought detailed orders and promises of British and American support. Gradually partisan bands were formed in the mountains. Military expertise was provided by Russian escaped prisoners of war. They were led by a Red Army captain known as 'Modena,' real name Viktor Pirogov.

The priest returned to the east coast and played a key role in operations to rescue Allied prisoners at large after the Armistice. He took part in dangerous missions to embark the men onto Allied vessels from a string of isolated beaches between Ancona and Pescara. These included Porto San Giorgio, San Benedetto del Tronto, Cupra Marritima and Giulia Nova.

The evacuation of 250 servicemen from the mouth of the River Menocchia was disrupted by the arrival of German gunboats. But an even larger number of prisoners were released in a daring raid on a holding camp at Fermo. Allied ships were called in to lay down an artillery barrage over the beach at Porta Civitanova to cover the fugitives' escape.

On 15 January 1944 Don Orlandini crossed the lines to the Maiella region of the Abruzzo. He returned with almost three hundred former prisoners. During the six months of the priest's involvement in the work, 3,700 Allied servicemen were rescued.

At the beginning of March, Don Orlandini took a parachutist training course at Gioia del Colle in Puglia. He was dropped with a team of saboteurs on a 40-day mission to the Le Marche region.

Then, as the periodical of the Green Flames, *'La Penna,'* records:

> Don Orlandini returned to be among the people and join their struggle against the invader. But at Tapignola he found only sadness and desolation. Don Borghi was gone, a victim of his own ideals, and the first partisan formations had disbanded after a roundup which spread terror throughout the zone. Cervarolo and Civago had been put to the torch and resurgent Fascism reigned supreme at Villa Minozzo.
>
> In the wild zone at the top of the Asta Valley, which was the second cradle of the partisan movement, a few brave men prepared to recommence the struggle. The victorious battle of Cerrè Sologno, in which Captain Miro [Riccardo Cocconi] was wounded, provided them with an omen that the partisan forces would succeed. 'Carlo,' joined them, sharing their poor food and the miserable straw beds of the mountain huts.

Don Orlandini had obtained the promise of supply drops from the Allies. He sent a message to confirm that operations could begin. The first mission was set for the night of 19 May. Large bonfires were lit as ground signals. To wild enthusiasm from the partisans, an aircraft released a shower of parachutes over the Asta Valley. The contents of the containers included 6 machine guns, 120 Stens and several boxes of hand-grenades and munitions.

Don Orlandini recalled subsequent events:

Towards the end of June, I managed to have with me a British Liaison Officer, Major Johnston, the best sort of person. He had studied at the University of Florence, spoke and understood Italian and also knew our mentality. Through his support, we were able to receive many airdrops at Ligonchio and in other zones.

We then moved to Villa Minozzo. Here I was made treasurer of the partisan brigades. The commandant was 'Miro' and the commissar, 'Eros' [Didimo Ferrari]. Numerous airdrops continued to arrive, as this zone, chosen by me and by Major Johnston, was to be a point of the greatest importance in the partisan resistance - it was to store the armaments for a battalion which would be parachuted into the area.

The Germans came to know of these plans and soon launched a roundup to ensure they failed. On one occasion while the airdrops were taking place it was reported that other aircraft were machine gunning and bombing the area. We have never been able to find out if this was a case of sabotage or if German planes had infiltrated the zone.

The material was collected and stored at Castiglione, near Asta. I advised 'Miro' against concentrating all the supplies in just one place for fear that in the event of a roundup they would all fall into enemy hands. In fact, I suggested hiding the goods in various mountain huts. But 'Miro' believed that the zone was virtually impregnable to the Germans.

Unfortunately, as I predicted, the German roundup arrived, employing troops particularly suited for anti-partisan warfare. [1]

Following the failure of Operation Albergo and the fall of the Republic of Montefiorino, the partisans gradually reformed and reorganised. With the support of the *Comando Unico*, Don Orlandini created a new unit, the *284th Brigata Fiamme Verdi*, the Green Flames.

The objective was straightforward: the expulsion of the enemy from Italian soil. Party propaganda was not allowed and political questions were shelved until the war was over. However, the Communists already had their own Garibaldi brigades. They had political commissars, red scarves and red stars, and the men sang Soviet songs. The Green Flames had none of these and appealed mainly to local Roman Catholics.

Despite understandable friction, the new brigade cooperated militarily with the Garibaldini under the coordination of the provincial military command. The Green Flames organised patrols, carried out sabotage, attacked enemy traffic and opposed German attempts to penetrate the partisan zone of Toano-Ligonchio-Villa Minozzo. The formation suffered its first losses in the battle of Cerré Marabino on 12 October 1944.

The great enemy offensive began in the province of Reggio Emilia on 7 January 1945. The Germans carried out a three-pronged attack in a vain attempt to encircle and annihilate the partisan brigades. In fierce fighting, the Green Flames lost their vice-commandant, Lieutenant Aldo Dall' Aglio, at Coriano on 10 January. The formation adopted his *nome di battaglia* of Italo. Aldo Dall' Aglio was posthumously awarded the Italian Silver Medal for Military Valour.

* * *

On Tuesday, 2 January 1945, the snow-covered drop zone above Case Balocchi, at the foot of Mount Cusna, received a new mission to relieve Major Johnston. In command was Captain Michael Lees, an experienced SOE agent, as we have already seen in Chapter 7. In Yugoslavia and northern Italy he had earned a reputation for coolness in action and an eagerness to carry the fight to the enemy.

The captain brought with him his wireless operator from the Flap 2 Mission near Turin, Bert Farrimond, who escaped from Piedmont after the partisans built the airfield at Vesime. The second-in-command was a Scot, Lieutenant Smith. The Envelope Mission was now solely attached to the Reggio Emilia partisan headquarters, while Silentia under Major Wilcockson covered Modena.

Five days later, the enemy offensive began. The agents had to move fast to avoid capture. When the enemy troops eventually withdrew, Michael Lees convened a meeting with the partisan provincial commandant, Colonel Monti (Augusto Berti), and the other leaders at Febbio.

A plan was agreed according to which, Mike Lees related:

> The partisans would be responsible to the *Comando Unico* as regards administrative matters, but for all operational questions, sabotage and tactical command, they would be responsible to me personally. All Intelligence would come direct to the mission. Political disturbances would not be tolerated. Finally, all brigades would be treated equally as purely military formations. Material from supply drops would be stored centrally and distributed fairly.

The mission established its base in the home of another priest, Don Pietro Rivi, in the village of Secchio. Michael Lees related that 'by establishing a definite and permanent HQ, intelligence was speeded up immeasurably, as all couriers always knew where to find the mission.' He added, 'I set about organising a sabotage squad and a private intelligence service.'

The captain asked an *Alpini* officer named Glauco Monducci (Gordon, after Flash Gordon) to build the 40-man sabotage team. He named it the *Gufo Nero* or Black Owl, seeing the nocturnal predator as the perfect symbol for the partisan who also had to live and survive in the mountains.

Intelligence was coordinated by a young partisan, Giulio Davoli (Kiss). He ran a team of *staffette*, or couriers, all girls in their teens and twenties. They not only carried messages and orders but also cycled into the towns and brought back detailed information on enemy strength and dispositions. The most famous courier was 'Noris,' Imelde Campani, who was aged 19 in 1945. She was awarded the Italian Bronze Medal for Military Valour in 1972.

On 6 February the Quartermaster at partisan HQ, Annibale Alpi, *Barbanera*, a former air force sergeant, began to build a new apolitical brigade on the orders of the colonel. It was known as the Military Formation.

Towards the end of the month, Special Force Tactical Headquarters asked the British Liaison Officers for their reaction to receiving an SAS company in their areas. The most enthusiastic response was from Captain Lees. He signalled: 'Send as many as you can!' Reggio was allocated the force.

The advance party of eight SAS men parachuted to the Case Balocchi field on Tuesday, 6 March, in Operation Tombola. Contrary to orders, they were led in person by Major Roy Farran (Major McGinty), commandant of 3 Squadron, 2 SAS. The official report said that he 'was helping dispatch the men from the door of one of the Dakotas, overbalanced and fell.' Fortunately, this assistant dispatcher was wearing a parachute. The major was billeted with the Envelope Mission in the priest's house at Secchio.

From 7 to 23 March an 'Allied Battalion' of 300 men was raised, equipped and trained in the valley. It consisted of three main elements.

A British SAS company, which grew to over 50 men, was based at the now deserted church at Tapignola. Attached to them were the *Gufo Nero* squad and 40 Garibaldini under Gianni Farri who were receiving heavy weapons training.

The Russian component was led by Red Army lieutenant Viktor Pirogov (Modena). He had escaped from a POW camp in Austria and became a partisan when there were only 20 in the whole valley. 'Modena' was tall, blond and handsome and inspired devotion amongst his men, most of whom were Mongol deserters from the 162nd Turkoman Infantry Division of the German Army.

Finally, there was the Italian Military Formation, to which British officers and weapons instructors were assigned.

Major Farran was the commandant of the Allied Battalion, with Annibale Alpi (*Barbanera*) as deputy and three company commanders: SAS Captain Jock Easton, Viktor Pirogov (Modena) and Remo Torlai (Tito). Outwardly the battalion was under the command of the *Comando Unico* and expected to receive rations and other assistance from it. Operationally the unit was independent.

Roy Farran recalled:

We did numerous small operations, but I should mention the largest and most significant:

(1) Together with the Garibaldini, we defended a bridge over the River Secchia from prolonged German attack.
(2) We attacked the German Corps HQ at Albinea.
(3) With the *Fiamme Verdi,* we successfully counter-attacked a German *rastrellamento* and drove them back out of our valley into the plains.
(4) In support of partisans from the Modena area, we carried out numerous attacks on the German supply line along

Highway 12, fought off another German counter-attack near Vallestra and Montefiorino, and finally shelled the retreating enemy columns north and west of Sassuolo. [2]

The formation carried out the audacious raid on the German Headquarters between 25 and 27 March 1945.

Mike Lees recalled:

> The Albinea attack was conceived by me at the end of February following a personal reconnaissance of the area and collection of intelligence from the GAP and SAP. I enthusiastically welcomed the offer of SAS help by Roy Farran and subsequently I was absolutely delighted (perhaps even a little relieved) when he made a surprise personal appearance on the stage and offered to take command. On 18 March aerial photographs were dropped to us and around 20 March the British mission received clearance to proceed with the attack. [3]

Led by Major Farran, a force of 24 SAS, 20 of the *Gufo Nero* squad, 20 Garibaldini and 30 Russians launched the attack on the Headquarters of the 51st German Mountain Corps, housed in two villas at Botteghe in the Commune of Albinea, only six miles south of Reggio.

On the second morning of the approach march, Major Farran received a curt message from Florence. He was ordered to postpone the assault for 10 days because there had been a change in plans for the main offensive. The major recalled: 'I resolved to pretend the signal failed to reach us in time. Though an attack on the corps headquarters might not have as much effect now as at the time of the main offensive, it would be infinitely better than no attack at all.'

Thirty Germans were killed in the raid, including the chief of staff, Colonel Lemelsen. By chance, the commanding artillery general of the 51st Mountain Corps, Friedrich-Wilhelm Hauck, was away on the night. The two main buildings of the headquarters were destroyed, together with many maps and papers.

There were three SAS fatalities: Lieutenant James Arthur Riccomini, MBE, MC, Sergeant Sidney Elliott Guscott, and Corporal Samuel Bolden, MM. Three other Britons were wounded and six partisans captured and five wounded. The injured included Captain Lees and 'Gordon.' They were saved by their comrades and with the help of local partisans eventually evacuated from Parma Province in the Special Force Fieseler Storch flown by Lieutenant Furio Lauri.

In 1987 Mike Lees told the conference held at Bologna University on 'No.1 Special Force and Italian Resistance':

The attack on the German HQ in Albinea in a highly defended zone must rank as one of the most ambitious, organised and daring operations carried out by the Resistance forces. One hundred men were infiltrated more than 30 miles down towards the plains and right inside a HQ directly defended by three hundred troops. What is more, after the action, apart from the three SAS heroes killed in the Villa Rossi, the entire party was got out again, sooner or later, without one single prisoner being taken by the Germans, thanks to the superb leadership of Roy Farran. It was a remarkable feat of arms, of organisation at every level, and above all of cooperation between the SAS under Roy Farran, the British Mission, the partisans from Reggio, the GAP and the SAP.

The concealment and subsequent rescue of Gordon (Glauco Monducci) and myself and the brilliant decision, taken I believe by Gianni Farri, to send us further into the plains towards Reggio - rather than into the foothills which were combed by the Germans - reflected enormous credit on the organisation and courage of the Resistance, of the many Italian civilians involved and of the two SAS troopers who helped carry us away.

Villa Rossi was more than a mere Corps HQ. Effectively it was Army TAC HQ. And Villa Calvi contained the main communications centre and direct telephone and teleprinter link with the *Reich* for all German Forces on that front. I had the good fortune to interview General Hauck in a POW camp near Riccione in 1947 and I know that the attack caused serious disruption to German control and morale apart from giving a very well deserved boost to the confidence of the Resistance. [4]

Like angry bees from an upturned hive, the enemy pursued the raiders back to their base. A mixed battalion of four hundred Germans and Mongols, equipped with mortars, two field guns and horse-drawn transport, penetrated the valley as far as Quara.

On Easter Sunday, 1 April, Major Farran found about 20 Green Flames on a small knoll two miles east of the village exchanging fire with Germans on a similar hillock two hundred yards away.

The major was heartened by the sudden arrival of the replacement British Liaison Officer, Captain John Lees (no relation to Michael), with

20 of his *Gufo Nero* squad. The two officers conferred and decided that only one course of action could save the day.

An urgent message was sent by runner to the Russians at Governara. 'Modena' arrived at the head of his troops after a three-hour forced march. He took readily to the idea of a counter-attack and deployed his men along the ridge.

Roy Farran described the final stage of what became known as the Battle of Ca' Marastoni - Monte della Castagna as follows:

The ragged line began to move behind me, slowly at first but gathering momentum all the time. The Russians cheered. Their loud hurrahs rang all along the crest and we moved down the slope in a shouting mob towards the enemy. I saw that Stephens and Taylor, who had also made several false starts, were moving them on the right. Our counter-attack was under way.

I may have been wrong - since I was so excited myself and tripped several times over stones, I might well have been - but our numbers seemed to swell. The Italians were particularly inspired by the charge and even outran the Russians, shooting wildly from the hip as they did so. Green Flames appeared from nowhere and, as we gathered momentum, I had the impression that the horde had grown to several hundreds.

It was such a fierce, unstoppable mob of yelling men that it was not surprising when the Germans broke and fled before we reached their positions. Red Very lights, presumably signals of distress or signals to retreat, went up from several points in front of us. I had started in the van but the pace was too much for me and I soon began to lag behind. However, I did see one episode. A group of Germans tried to make a stand in a farmhouse, but the excited partisans ran straight through their bullets, firing from the hip, pumping tracers into the windows. A Green Flame carrying a Bren led a crowd of yelling Russians up to the building. He fired point blank through the window and several Germans came out with their hands up. Two, I remember, were wearing unusual white tunics. The partisans shot them down without mercy. I heard later that two other prisoners were dreadfully mutilated by the Russians, but am unable to say whether the report was true.

It was obvious from the signal flares that the Germans were much more widely dispersed than I had imagined. But it was also clear that they were in full retreat everywhere. I struggled on, trying to keep up with the charge. Our men were now utterly beyond control and I only hoped that the Germans would not attempt to stand on our side of the river. But there was no need to fear. Throwing away their arms, the enemy ran panic-stricken northwards.

For the first time the Reggio partisans had defeated a German battalion. Roy Farran concluded: 'By nightfall, not a single enemy soldier remained alive on our side of the Secchia. It was an accomplishment that surprised me no less than the enemy.' [5]

The Green Flames were ordered by the *Comando Unico* to descend on the city as the advancing Allies neared the border of the province. The *284th Brigata Fiamme Verdi 'Italo'* now consisted of five hundred partisans organised into three battalions, an autonomous detachment and five squads.

By the morning of 24 April most of the brigade were at the gates of the city. They helped the advance guard of the 5th Army to flush out the last German and Fascist resistance. At 4.30pm the Green Flames entered Reggio, the first of the mountain brigades to do so, and they hoisted the tricolour flag on the City Hall.

After receiving new airdrops of jeeps and a 75mm Howitzer, the Allied Battalion transferred to the Modena Valley and attacked retreating German columns on Route 12 until the end of the war.

Following the Victory Parade in Modena, the Russian auxiliaries were disarmed and ordered to a holding camp, ready for deportation. Most met a cruel fate in Stalin's Russia. However, their leader, 'Modena,' simply vanished. He was rumoured to have opened a small dress shop in Milan.

Roy Farran recalled the aftermath of Operation Tombola:

Fortunately, I did not receive a trial by court-martial as I expected. The British faction that wanted to try me on two counts - for parachuting behind the lines when forbidden to do so and for attacking the German headquarters at Albinea in contravention of orders - was narrowly defeated, largely through support I received from Colonel Riepe, the US officer at Fifteenth Army Group in charge of special operations. He even went so far as to recommend me for a US Legion of Merit - an ace in the hole because I could hardly be court martialled for something for which I had been decorated.

His citation concerning Operation Tombola said that our operations against enemy rear units south of Modena materially assisted the attack of the United States Fourth Corps and contributed significantly to the success of Fifteenth Army Group.

Who dares wins. [6]

Roy Farran became one of the most highly decorated soldiers of World War II. As well as the American Legion of Merit, he was awarded the British DSO and the MC with two Bars, and the French *Croix de Guerre*.

The Green Flames were demobilised on 3 May 1945. 'Don Carlo' told his men:

> We deposit our weapons, every one of us resuming our place in life. With the same enthusiasm with which we have destroyed a vile state, we will build a new one, strong and ready to serve everyone, especially the poor. Farewell.

* * *

We began our story with Operation Baytown, the attack across the Straits of Messina by 8th Army. The General Officer Commanding, Lieutenant General Richard McCreery, sent this congratulatory message to his troops six days before the end of the conflict:

> You have played a decisive part in this great Eighth Army offensive. You have driven the enemy north of the River Po in disorder. You have all shown a splendid determination and fighting spirit, and a fine endurance in two and a half weeks of continuous battle. Your attack across the River Senio, so carefully prepared, succeeded so well that the enemy was unable to stand on the River Santerno. After capturing bridgeheads over this river, you exploited rapidly northwards, and in combination with outflanking operations executed with great skill along the shores of Lake Comacchio, you succeeded in forcing the formidable Argenta position. The enemy was protected by extensive floods on both flanks and by deep minefields covering the gaps, but you attacked him by day and night and broke out into the more open country towards Ferrara. This success was decisive for the whole plan of operations of Fifteenth Army Group.
>
> Your subsequent determined and relentless advance to the River Po, both east and west of Ferrara, drove the enemy back over the river with heavy losses in tanks, guns, motorised

transport and equipment. Only remnants of his fighting units succeeded in escaping, and our aim to destroy the enemy south of the river has been largely successful.

All Arms have played an equally important part in this great victory. Good leadership has resulted in the close cooperation between the infantry, tanks, artillery and engineers, which is the secret of success.

I send my warmest congratulations to every man in 5 Corps. I know that you will continue a relentless pursuit to finish off the enemy and to prevent him organising on any further defensive line.

On 29 April 1945 a German peace delegation arrived at Allied Headquarters at Caserta in southern Italy. Secret discussions on a possible surrender had been held in Switzerland over the previous two months between SS General Karl Wolff and Allen Dulles, OSS station head. Preservation of 'military honour' was the main German concern.

Lieutenant General Victor von Schweinitz and SS Major Max Wenner were authorised to conduct negotiations and make binding commitments on behalf of the new German commander, General Heinrich von Vietinghoff, and General Wolff. The officers said they also had the approval of Marshal Rodolfo Graziani, Fascist War Minister, to include the Republican Army in any agreement.

At 2pm the delegates signed the document of unconditional surrender. Other Germans accused them of treachery and ordered their arrest. These attempts failed as rival commanders fought for power. The cease-fire came into effect on 2 May. The war in Italy was over.

And the sequel: in the words of the poet, 'Bliss was it in that dawn to be alive, but to be young was very heaven.'

NOTES

[1] Don Domenico Orlandini quoted in the book by Luca Pallaj, *Storia della 284a Brigata Fiamme Verdi 'Italo'*, pp 32-3.
[2] Roy Farran, 'The British Mission to Reggio Emilia,' *No. 1 Special Force and Italian Resistance*, pp 213-14.
[3] Michael Lees, 'The Attack on Villa Rosi,' *No. 1 Special Force and Italian Resistance*, p 218.
[4] Ibid., pp 217-18.
[5] Roy Farran, *Operation Tombola*, pp 138-140.
[6] Ibid., pp 255-6.

Bibliography

Battaglia, Roberto, *The Story of the Italian Resistance*, London: Odhams Press, 1957.

Churchill, Winston S, *The Second World War, Volume V, Closing the Ring*, London: Penguin Books, 1985.

Corvo, Max, *The O.S.S. in Italy 1942-1945, A Personal Memoir*, New York: Praeger Publishers, 1990.

Farran, Roy, *Operation Tombola*, London: Arms and Armour Press, 1986.

Foot, Michael, *SOE, Special Operations Executive 1940-1946*, London: Pimlico, 1999.

Lamb, Richard, *War in Italy 1943-1945, A Brutal Story*, London: Penguin Books, 1995.

Langrishe, John, *The Long Walk Out*, private circulation, 1994.

Lett, Gordon, *Rossano (An Adventure of the Italian Resistance)*, London: Hodder and Stoughton, 1955. Republished by Brian Gordon Lett, 2001.

Lewis, Laurence, *Echoes of Resistance, British Involvement with the Italian Partisans*, Tunbridge Wells: Costello, 1985.

Macintosh, Charles, DSO, *From Cloak to Dagger, An SOE Agent in Italy 1943-1945*, London: William Kimber, 1982.

Mackenzie, William, *The Secret History of SOE, Special Operations Executive 1940-1945*, London: St Ermin's Press, 2002.

Merrick, Kenneth, *Flights of the Forgotten, Special Duties Operations in World War Two*, London: Arms and Armour Press, 1989.

Minardi, Marco & Storchi, Massimo, eds., *Messaggi dall' Emilia, Le missioni n. 1 Special Force e l'attività d'intelligence in Emilia, 1944-1945*, Parma: Istituto Storico della Resistenza e dell' età contemporanea di Parma, 2003.

Pallaj, Luca (Donato), *Storia della 284a Brigata Fiamme Verdi 'Italo,'* Reggio Emilia: Edizione ALPI, 1970.

Tudor, Malcolm, *British Prisoners of War in Italy: Paths to Freedom*, Newtown: Emilia Publishing, 2000.

Tudor, Malcolm, *Escape from Italy, 1943-45, Allied Escapers and Helpers in Fascist Italy*, Newtown: Emilia Publishing, 2003.

Tudor, Malcolm, *Special Force: SOE and the Italian Resistance 1943-1945*, Newtown: Emilia Publishing, 2004.

Tudor, Malcolm, *Prisoners and Partisans: Escape and Evasion in World War II Italy*, Newtown: Emilia Publishing, 2006.

Various authors, *Gli Americani e la Guerra di Liberazione in Italia, Office of Strategic Services (OSS) e la Resistenza Italiana*, Rome: Presidenza del Consiglio dei Ministri, 1995.

Various authors, *No. 1 Special Force and Italian Resistance, n. 1 Special Force nella Resistenza italiana*, Bologna: University of Bologna, 1990.

Index of Names

Sanini, A 24n
'Scalabrino' (partisan) 109
Schweinitz, von, V 142
Sebastian (escaper) 18-19
Shindler, H 79
Simon, M 105-6
Slessor, J, Sir 63
Smith, Lieutenant 109, 134
Sogno, E 72
Spaatz, CA 61-3
Stawell, WA 64
Steed, W (Bill) 78-9
Steeds, S 80
Stephens (SAS) 139
Stevens, J 74, 76
Stewart, 'Red' 43
Storm, A and R 79-82
Stott, J 95

Tarchiani, A 54
Taylor (SAS) 139
Torlai, R ('Tito') 136
Tudor, KW vii
Turner, J 41

Urry, S 80

Vallesi, P 80
Van Eysenn, JL 77
Vaughan-Fowler, P 77
Venieri, L 80
Vicedomini, E 2
Victor Emmanuel III, King 54, 56, 58n, 70
Vietinghoff, von, H 142

Wenner, M 142
Wilcockson, EH 89-98, 109, 119, 128, 134
Wilson, M 63
Wolff, K 142

Woods, C 68